Better Homes and Gardens®

ADDING ON

BETTER HOMES AND GARDENS® BOOKS

Editor: Gerald M. Knox
Art Director: Ernest Shelton
Managing Editor: David A. Kirchner

Associate Art Directors: Linda Ford Vermie,
Neoma Alt West, Randall Yontz
Copy and Production Editors: Marsha Jahns,
Mary Helen Schiltz, Carl Voss, David A. Walsh
Assistant Art Directors: Harijs Priekulis, Tom Wegner
Senior Graphic Designers: Alisann Dixon, Lynda Haupert,
Lyne Neymeyer
Graphic Designers: Mike Burns, Mike Eagleton, Deb Miner,
Stan Sams, D. Greg Thompson, Darla Whipple, Paul Zimmerman

Vice President, Editorial Director: Doris Eby
Group Editorial Services Director: Duane L. Gregg

General Manager: Fred Stines
Director of Publishing: Robert B. Nelson
Vice President, Retail Marketing: Jamie Martin
Vice President, Direct Marketing: Arthur Heydendael

All About Your House: Adding On

Project Editor: James A. Hufnagel
Associate Editor: Willa Rosenblatt Speiser
Assistant Editor: Leonore A. Levy
Copy and Production Editor: Mary Helen Schiltz
Building and Remodeling Editor: Joan McCloskey
Furnishings and Design Editor: Shirley Van Zante
Garden Editor: Douglas A. Jimerson
Money Management and Features Editor: Margaret Daly

Associate Art Director: Linda Ford Vermie
Graphic Designer: Paul Zimmerman
Electronic Text Processor: Cynthia Kalwishky McClanahan

Contributing Editor: Dan Kaercher
Contributing Senior Writer: Paul Kitzke
Contributors: Lawrence D. Clayton, Jim Harrold,
Jill Abeloe Mead, Stephen Mead, Peter J. Stephano

Special thanks to William N. Hopkins, Bill Hopkins, Jr.,
Babs Klein, and Don Wipperman for their valuable
contributions to this book.

ADDING
ON

INTRODUCTION

When a house feels too snug for comfort, it's exciting to think about expanding with a new room or two. As you'll discover in photograph after photograph on the pages that follow, a well-planned addition can do wonders for a home's livability. But before you get carried away with what a new family room, kitchen, or master suite could offer, stop and ask yourself a few hard questions.

First and foremost: Does it really make sense for your family, your house, your neighborhood, and your finances to invest in an addition? *Adding On* tackles this question in the very first chapter and continues to address it throughout the book.

If, for whatever reason, an addition *doesn't* seem right for your situation, *Adding On* still might be able to ease your space squeeze. Perhaps some clever furnishing schemes can solve the problem. Or perhaps you can add "in" by developing an attic, porch, or garage, or by reshaping existing interior spaces. You'll find chapters about both of these subjects, too.

If you do decide to add on, what are your options? How do you go about planning an addition? What's involved in building one? Where can you find the money to pay for it? How can you make a good architectural match with your existing house? And what about legal and long-term financial considerations?

Planning and building even a small addition is one of the biggest jobs a homeowner is likely to take on—trickier in many ways than planning an entirely new house. *Adding On* takes you step by step through the entire process, from those initial questions and ideas through the finished and furnished end result. Drawings, floor plans, charts, and more than 150 color photographs show what could happen at your house if an addition adds up for you.

Adding On is one in a series of books in the **ALL ABOUT YOUR HOUSE** library, a wide-ranging encyclopedia of home planning, decorating, building, and management from Better Homes and Gardens. Other volumes delve with equal thoroughness into other aspects of your home.

CONTENTS

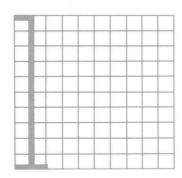

WOULD ADDING ON MAKE SENSE FOR YOU?

Somehow, your house just isn't working right. It seems too small, but a look at the monthly payments that buying a bigger house would entail has convinced you to stay put. Maybe you don't want to leave the neighborhood, or you value the local schools. Any or all of these might justify adding on to your present home. But there are also some persuasive factors that could argue against an addition. This introductory chapter examines both the pros and cons of adding on. Use it to evaluate whether your home is a good candidate for an addition and, if so, what you ought to build.

DO YOU REALLY NEED AN ADDITION?

Just because your family is feeling pinched for space doesn't necessarily mean you should commit yourself to a costly new room (or rooms). Maybe, instead of an addition, your house would fit better with just a nip here and a tuck there.

Skillful decorating, for instance, can help rooms look—and live—bigger than you might imagine. Chapter 2—"Furnishing and Decorating Solutions to Space Problems"—tells how playing with scale, changing rooms' roles, subdividing, and a half-dozen other decorating ploys could ease the squeeze at your house.

Also ask yourself if every area of your home is living up to its potential. Example: The homeowners pictured *at right* needed a family room, handy to the kitchen, where they could gather with their three children. A porch off the dining room provided a roof and floor for the new room; building well-insulated walls and installing a heat-circulating fireplace turned summer-only space into a cozy, year-round living area.

No porch at your house? How about the basement, attic, or an attached garage? Or maybe you can gain precious space by rearranging walls and ceilings. Chapter 3—"Adding In"—examines six practical, popular alternatives to adding on.

Perhaps you're already convinced that an addition offers the only way to gain the space your family needs. If so, now it's time to take a careful look at your house itself, your family's needs, and your resources.

WOULD ADDING ON MAKE SENSE FOR YOU?

DOES ADDING ON MAKE ECONOMIC SENSE?

Entering a long-term relationship with a house is like picking a mate: Most of us aren't very objective at first. Maybe you've fallen in love with the pine trees out front, or the oak woodwork, or the bay window. Later, shortcomings seem to crop up. The bedrooms turn out to be too small, perhaps, or there isn't enough storage space, or the basement is damp and dreary. Before you commit yourself to adding on, take a long, hard second look at your house, lot, and neighborhood. Are they worth a major investment of time and money?

To critically appraise your house, act as if you were house hunting all over again. Like any prospective buyer, ask yourself these questions.

• *How's your home's physical condition?* Are its mechanical systems—electrical, plumbing, and heating/cooling—up to date? What's the condition of the roof and exterior? How about interior walls and floors, the basement and foundation? Is the house well insulated and reasonably energy efficient?

If any of your home's major elements have seen better days, consider upgrading these first—or selling your house and buying another.

• *Do you have space for an addition?* If you're shoehorned into a tight city lot, or drydocked on a steep-sloping site, adding on may at first seem physically impossible. But before you give up, check Chapter 4—"A Portfolio of Addition Alternatives"—for ways to add on that you might not have considered. While you're thinking about where an addition might best be located, bear in mind that zoning ordinances may have a lot to say about the answer. Pages 134-137 explain what you need to know about zoning.

• *How's the neighborhood?* Is the community relatively stable, starting to slide, or on the rebound? How about your neighbors, the schools, the shopping, and distances to work? Would an addition overprice your house for the neighborhood, or send your property taxes soaring? If you rate your neighborhood favorably in most of these areas, fine. If not, maybe you should be looking around rather than adding on.

WHAT ARE YOUR RESOURCES?

Adding on, like any major building project, raises two related questions: Who's going to do the work, and how much will the project cost? The answers depend on your finances, building skills, and one other resource—willing and able do-it-yourselfers who can be called upon to help you with critical parts of the construction process. Here's how to evaluate these resources.

Even if you already have one or several sizable do-it-yourself projects under your belt, think carefully before deciding to build an entire addition on your own. Interior projects—such as finishing an attic or basement, moving walls, even remodeling a kitchen—are, for the most part, one-person projects. Constructing an addition, on the other hand, is more like building a new house. You have to excavate, lay a foundation or footings, frame in the structure, and complete its exterior shell before you even get to the point where interior projects begin.

What's more, the work you do must satisfy community building codes and conform with generally accepted standards of construction. Add to this the fact that many lenders look questioningly at amateur add-ons, and you may well decide to hand the job over to professionals.

With savvy and a little help from others, though, it is possible to pull off a major addition

project all or mostly on your own. The one shown here is a case in point. The owners first had a professional excavate and pour a slab for their new room. Then they ordered framing and sheathing materials and rounded up a stalwart crew of friends and neighbors to participate in a modern-day barn-raising. Framing in the new space and enclosing it from the elements took one weekend; completing exterior finish work took another. Then the owners soloed through the remainder of the project, calling on others only from time to time.

To learn about the major stages involved in adding on, see Chapter 6—"Building an Addition." For advice about codes, contractors, architects, budgeting, and financing, check Chapter 5—"Planning Your Addition"—and Chapter 9—"Practical Matters."

HOW MUCH SPACE DO YOU NEED, WHERE—AND WHAT KIND?

After you've determined that your house is a good candidate for an addition, and that you probably have the resources to build one, it's time to zero in on design considerations. How big should your addition be? Where should it go? What shape should you add? What special features should you include? For the best answers to these questions, you might want to turn to an architect or other design professional.

Though it measures only 13x5 feet, the high-rising attic addition shown *at left* transformed a merely adequate master bedroom into an airy retreat. It's an example of a successful single-purpose addition made special thanks to unusual architectural features, such as tall Palladian windows, a vaulted ceiling, and a built-in bed platform.

Even if you intend to do all or most of the construction work yourself—or already have a contractor in mind—a design professional can help you develop a plan that truly works well for your family's needs. Pages 66-73 explain how a professional designer operates, taking you from preliminary meetings through the preparation of rough sketches, completed working drawings, and materials specifications.

Experienced designers often think of features you might not have considered. For example, the owners of the home shown *above* needed more kitchen and eating space. Their architect proposed a greenhouse-style bump-out that serves as an informal family sitting room as well as a delightful dining area.

An architect or other design professional also can assure that your addition will harmonize with the rest of the house—a critical consideration in any adding-on project. Chapter 7—''Fitting In''— explains the aesthetic and functional considerations involved in successfully blending the new with the old.

Finally, now—at the initial design phase—is the time to plan finishing touches that can make an addition special. Chapter 10 presents more than a dozen ideas you might want to borrow.

WOULD ADDING ON MAKE SENSE FOR YOU?

Now that you have a handle on what you need, what you can afford, and where it should go, give careful thought to what adding on would do for (or to) the rest of your home's layout. If your home has a plan problem, perhaps the addition could unsnarl it; certainly you don't want to add new space that would turn a perfectly good floor plan into a disorienting maze of rooms. The key factors here are zoning (not, this time, community ordinances, but rather the way areas in a house are grouped by function) and traffic patterns (the ways people move to or through one area to another).

HOW WOULD ADDING ON AFFECT YOUR HOME'S PLAN?

Start your evaluation by studying your home's original floor plan (if it's available) or by sketching a rough plan on graph paper. Then analyze what would happen to it if you were to build the addition you're thinking about.

Divide your house into living, sleeping, and working zones, bearing in mind that some overlap is inevitable. Working zones—garage, laundry, kitchen, and utility rooms—are the noisiest, busiest, and usually the messiest in the house. Separate them as best you can from living zones, but keep kitchen access in mind for dining areas. For example, the 24x13-foot addition shown *at left* brought new livability for a family with young children. Located at the back of the house, the new dining/family room clears clutter from more formal rooms at the front of the house and keeps the kids in touch with the kitchen.

Take buffers into account, especially if you're adding bedrooms. Sleeping zones should be private and quiet, with easy access to bathrooms and clothes storage. Closets, stairways, and built-in storage units are highly effective sound filters.

Now look at how traffic will flow. For example, what's the shortest route from the garage or driveway to the kitchen? This is one you have to traverse with bags of groceries. Will guests step directly from the front door into your living room, or can you provide an entry of some sort? How about bathrooms? One or more should be located within easy range of the bedrooms, of course, but a half-bath near main living areas and the family entry will minimize traffic traipsing through sleeping zones.

WOULD ADDING ON MAKE SENSE FOR YOU?

Congratulations! If you've followed our short course on evaluating, you're ready to finalize a plan of action. You know whether you need to add in or add on and what you want the addition to accomplish. You've decided whether to do the work yourself, hire a contractor, or combine forces. Now it's time to start interviewing people, considering materials, and turning the idea into reality. If you've done your homework, you'll be reaping the benefits at your house for years to come.

WHAT SHOULD YOU DO BEFORE WORK BEGINS?

For this last preliminary phase of building an addition, you'll need a pencil, lots of paper, a telephone, enough time and energy to do some legwork, and plenty of patience. Before you begin, make sure you haven't lost sight of the needs that triggered the addition in the first place. Study the overall design and how well it fits in with the existing house. Review traffic flow, energy efficiency, storage, finances, mechanical systems, and all the other elements that will contribute to the success of your addition.

Now get out the pencil and paper and start making phone calls. If you don't plan to do the work yourself, ask friends and relatives for the names of reliable architects and contractors, then ask them for bids, as explained on pages 72 and 73 and pages 138 and 139.

Regardless of who does the work, you'll need to visit building supply centers to scout for special materials and components such as fixtures, cabinets, flooring, and exterior finish items. (Chapter 8—"Exterior Surface Materials"—tells what you need to know about siding and roofing materials and paints and stains.) Be sure to keep an accurate tab of prices, model numbers, sizes, and other relevant data, and to order everything you need well in advance. Little is more frustrating than to have workers standing around wasting expensive time because what arrived isn't what you wanted—or something didn't arrive at all.

After all your choices have been made, and just before the first workers arrive, move furniture out of the way and protect the rest of the house from dust and debris. Then stand back and let the hammers fly!

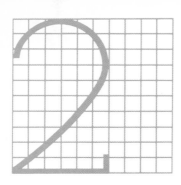

FURNISHING AND DECORATING SOLUTIONS TO SPACE PROBLEMS

Suffering from a space shortage? Before you leap to the conclusion that your house needs an addition, take another look. Maybe all that's really required is to rework space you already have. With the right furnishings and decorating, even tiny areas can be made to function in big ways. This chapter explores how color, scale, and other design ploys enlarge a room visually. To help ease the physical squeeze, we also include tips on built-ins, multipurpose furnishings, and other space-making strategies.

PLAY WITH SCALE

Properly manipulated, scale—the relationship between an object and the space around it—can uncramp even closet-size quarters. The *visual* size of a piece of furniture or accessory often belies its *actual* size, which means you can use a lot of furniture, as long as the pieces themselves are visually light in weight, and in proper proportion to one another and to the size of your room. For example, chairs with open arms (or none at all) are visual "lightweights"; the entire room can be seen through them. Sofas lose visual weight when they shed their skirts. Upholstery or window treatment fabrics that blend with background color tend to look less heavy, too. Reflective or transparent surfaces (glass, chrome, mirrors) open up a room.

Also manipulate scale by balancing one "heavyweight" with a group of objects. Two chairs and an end table will balance a sofa or love seat. Cut a massive bank of shelves to scale with small, stored shapes like books, baskets, or bottles.

In the living room *at right*, small space has been stretched to achieve maximum comfort in a setting of cozy elegance. The fireplace, a natural focal point, is balanced by the comfortable but unskirted love seat. Two open-arm rattan chairs are see-through in effect; the clear glass lamp base is literally transparent. A mirror adds visual space to the room and amplifies the light pouring through space-saving mini-blinds. Big plants claim little precious floor space, but add to the overall impression of airy spaciousness.

FURNISHING AND DECORATING SOLUTIONS

SWITCH ROOMS

Want to move rooms without tearing out walls or adding expensive square feet? Maybe all you need to do is give different jobs to the rooms you have. An awkward hallway also might serve as a mini-office. An extra bedroom might become the den your family needs—or vice versa. Room switching is an easy and fun way to "add" living space.

Before you raise clouds of costly remodeling dust, cast a creatively pragmatic eye around your home. Search out "useless" or underused spaces and put them to work. Creating living space you need from underused space you didn't realize you had makes better use of the room your home offers.

Evaluating your family's space needs (see Chapter 1) may have disclosed that your life-style doesn't fit your floor plan. If you live casually, and prefer meals in the kitchen, a formal dining room may be underused. The room *opposite* was such a dining space.

A simple switch produced this much-needed, much-used "new" family room for television, reading, and relaxing.

Now the family eats in the kitchen most of the time, but they found a space to put to excellent use for more formal dining. The basement room *above* was once just a nice place to dump things. Now, warm-white paint on the rough stone walls and open-joist ceiling, Early American-style furnishings, textured woven rugs, and glowing candlelight transformed this formerly useless basement space into a quaint, convivial dining room.

SUBDIVIDE

Need another room? Consider this idea: Divide before you add. When a room is subdivided either physically or visually, each area can serve a different purpose, so that one room functions as two or more.

Often you can physically subdivide space with a single structure. In the bedroom/study shown here, the divider is a freestanding wall, built below ceiling level to let in sunlight from the bedroom's bay window.

On the study side (out of camera range), a love seat is flanked with reading lamps, fronted by a coffee table, and faced by a small desk. Floor-to-ceiling wall-hung bookshelves complete the study.

Drawers line the sleep side of the miniwall. The drawers, a freestanding chest (set away from the window to let in maximum daylight), a walk-in closet, and the built-in headboard provide ample storage. (More about built-ins on pages 30 and 31.) The bed is set on a recessed base so it seems to "float"—a visual lightweight, topped with an antique quilt. Although the function of each area is different, a light, white background provides a decorative sense of unity.

In many instances, you don't need any structure at all to subdivide a space. One old standby, the screen, can be updated with paint, fabric, or a stencil design. For an airier divider, use a large potted plant, like a ficus, with a grouping of smaller plants arranged at its base. Or place a big piece of furniture—a piano, perhaps— at right angles to the wall to mark off boundaries.

Achieve visual divisions with a change of color scheming. On bare floors or wall-to-wall carpet, delineate spaces with area rugs.

Use area rugs also to *unify* the entire room and make the living space more pleasurable. Other unifiers are upholstery fabrics repeated from "room" to "room," similar window treatments, and a one-color background.

PUT COLOR TO WORK

The human eye can perceive countless colors, and the human soul delights in them. We give them evocative names, like tomato red, lemon yellow, apricot, avocado. We are all emotionally affected by color: Serene blue calms us, red fires us up. Make no mistake, color affects us all, whether we're aware of it or not. Happily, it can work *for* us, too. Once you know that light or cool colors can be used to expand space and warm or dark ones to shrink it, you'll reach for the hardest-working, easiest-to-use, least expensive way to add color available—paint.

Even if you think you're limited by inexperience or time, you can work miracles with paint. Just as you can rescale furniture with color, you can open up a small room with light color on the ceiling—and all around, as was done with many of the rooms shown in this chapter.

Now let's pull a switch on that basic small-room color rule. Covering the walls of a bedroom alcove or a small dining area with *dark* paint sets them off—an easy, dramatic way to subdivide.

Make the most of paint finishes, too. Add impact to a small area—or define it more sharply—by covering walls with finishes that range from flat to highly glossy. Don't overlook shiny lacquers that can pump new vigor into tired furniture or bring dazzling color to a plain wall. Textured paint can disguise slightly imperfect plaster, negating the need for costly wallpaper or repair.

Paint is so versatile that your biggest problem may be choosing from the wide variety of colors. The living room *at left* shows the results of following two simple guidelines.
- White plus one other major color is a foolproof scheme.
- A color scheme can be "borrowed" from a painting.

Here, sunny yellow paint covers the walls. For contrast, the space is liberally laced with areas of crisp white on the ceiling, woodwork, and in the area rug. Aqua, tangerine, and peach accents in the room echo those in the paintings and avoid any danger of things becoming too monochromatic. The bright colors and crisp textures are balanced by the dramatic textural "stripes" underfoot and the natural warmth of an eclectic mix of accessories.

25

TRY MIRRORS

Mirrors are magic. They sparkle and reflect, brightening any room. Mirror one whole wall to "double" a room, or mirror parts of several walls and multiply the dazzle. Use sections of walls mirrored floor-to-ceiling to create "windows" of light or pleasing reflections. Use colored mirrors—silver, sleek smoky gray, warm copper or bronze—to establish mood. Frame smaller mirrors and hang them singly or in groups to open up an entry and reflect the next room.

Imagine a mirror wherever you wish and rest assured that you'll be able to find a shape, size, or style to meet your needs. A professional can custom-cut and install standard plate mirror panels, or you can easily fit mirrors yourself by using inexpensive 12-inch squares of mirror tile with self-sticking backing. Or try mirror strips, which are available in a variety of lengths, widths, and colors. Squares and strips have an advantage in addition to ease of application—fewer mirrors achieve much the same expansive qualities as a total covering does.

Just how expansive those qualities can be is apparent in the living room *at right*. Replacing an old fireplace mantel with mirror panels effectively rescales this 12x24-foot room, neatly doubling its visual depth. The reflective surface breaks up the longest wall and helps shrink the room's tunnel-like proportions. White cotton-covered seating pieces and jet black accents become even more dramatic when mirrored in the fireplace facade.

Whatever you're mirroring, be sure that it's worth seeing twice. Placing furniture away from a mirrored wall furthers the mirror's expansive powers—a good trick if the back sides of the pieces in question are as attractive as their fronts.

Just one caution: Mirrors can make awkward corners and columns magically "vanish". Take care that your effects aren't so bewildering that they cause people to walk into them.

EXPLORE MULTIPURPOSE FURNISHINGS

Why use valuable space for two or three pieces of furniture when one multipurpose version will serve just as well? Some multipurpose items, like the Murphy bed which folds up and away into the wall during off-duty time, have been around for years. Others are new—incorporating new ideas, new materials, new looks, and new efficiency. Still others cleverly combine old ideas and modern-day techniques.

The cozy dining room *above* and sleek hallway *opposite* are the same— and a dramatic example of how multifunction furnishings can work for you. The handsome drop-leaf dining table spends most of its time as a hall piece, providing a convenient drop-off place for mail and packages. Its hidden assets include four chairs stored neatly inside. At dinnertime, the chairs come out, the table is repositioned, and the space assumes its new identity.

That's just the beginning. For example, those old standbys, the brass-bound chest and the wicker trunk, are as versatile as ever. They're good both for storage and as end tables, and they set a distinctive decorative mood, too.

The convertible sofa is another time-honored spacesaver. In fact, the concept is so popular that nowadays chairs and even chests also convert to beds.

Conversely, mattresses double as sit-upon furniture more gracefully than you might think. Bright fitted bed coverings and striking throw pillows turn a bed into a sofa overnight.

New multipurpose ideas include clean-lined plastic modular drawers that stack into chests, headboards, and bed platforms anywhere where extra space is needed.

When you need to make more out of the space you have, see what's available ready-made. More and more manufacturers, designers, and homeowners are finding ways to use wasted space. If you don't find what you need, you may very well be able to put two and two together and get six on your own.

BUILD IN

Let's consider clutter. Has yours got you climbing the wall? Backed into a corner? Built-ins can climb those walls for you. They can also hide in a corner behind the door (and in other slivers of wasted space), ready to capture clutter. Freeing up floor space opens up a room to an astonishing degree, and built-ins can do that with flair.

If the only available open space in a room is closer to the ceiling than the floors, reclaim it with built-in storage that stretches from floor to ceiling. Hide whatever you want behind doors, or leave shelves open to keep objects on display.

Corners also are good places to flex your creativity. Even a tiny empty corner in your kitchen may be large enough for a simple triangular built-in counter. Add two bar stools and you've gained eating space. Add shelves and gain a desk.

Built-ins take naturally to "underdeveloping," too—use them to take advantage of undeveloped spaces below stairs or windows. A small, hidable office or sewing room with built-in shelves and a well-lighted work surface can fit into below-stairs space. On a more modest scale, build in seats under bay or dormer windows with foam-topped, fabric-shirred plywood; then add built-in storage below.

Nooks, crannies, and niches make inviting hideaways. With built-ins, they can be that and more. The low-ceilinged attic bedroom *at left* retains its cozy feeling but is a great space-extender. A small desk tucks into a sweep of built-in storage units in one nook; another unit houses a bed that also does double-duty as a daytime seating area. The warm but clear-lined color scheme and well-conceived floor plan make this room at the top tops.

STREAMLINE

Here's another way you can get more living from limited floor space: Subtract to add. When you strip all nonessential furnishings from a room, you free it of clutter—and free yourself from excessive day-to-day maintenance. Streamlining furniture, accessories, floors, and windows reclaims both visual and actual space.

If the purpose of a room is conversation, but homework papers, a television set, and an overflowing sewing basket seem to be taking over, the room is a likely candidate for streamlining. The same goes for a room that's tidy enough, but crowded with furniture, busy patterns on upholstery or floor covering, or fussy window treatments.

This doesn't mean you should junk cherished objects or those that are used only part of the time. To ease living, consider moving them to one gloriously *un*streamlined room.

Pare down furniture as you do smaller items—by similar thoughtful culling, by rescaling, or by replacing several single-function pieces with one multi-purpose piece. Remember that built-ins can free up floor space—and provide space for storage or display.

Strip down floors, too. Keep them understated: painted, polished, or bleached bare wood; unobtrusive wall-to-wall carpet. Fade windows into the background by leaving them totally uncovered. If privacy is required, opt for minimal-look blinds, shades, or shutters.

As the living room *at right* shows, streamlining need not result in a sterile look—even with a stripped down "noncolor" scheme. Here, a white wall, shiny ceramic floor tiles, and smooth-textured cotton duck upholstery, made more dramatic by the contrasting dark walls, set a serene stage for good conversations before a cheery fire. A wine rack, television, and stereo system are at hand behind doors in the fireplace wall at the left of our photo.

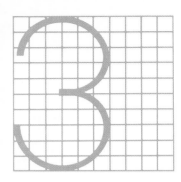

ADDING
IN

You've had it. Your house simply doesn't measure up anymore. What once seemed like a comfortably large home is now so irritatingly small that you have no place to turn and no room to move. What's the answer? A new addition? Perhaps. But before you decide, take a closer look around. You may discover undeveloped territory —an attic, basement, porch, or garage—just waiting to become part of the family. With careful planning, adding in can add up to the extra living space you need. This chapter will show you likely places to look.

BY FINISHING YOUR ATTIC

Here's a top-drawer solution: If your attic has enough headroom (at least 10 feet at the peak), convert it into living space. The one shown *at right,* designed within existing roof lines, is a striking example. The ponderosa pine paneling, with plank floors stained to match, helps make this adult retreat the ultimate in cozy luxury.

Follow this advice when you're considering finishing your attic:
• Gaining access may be your biggest problem. Plan at least a 3x10-foot rectangle for a standard stairway or a 5½-foot square for a spiral unit. To make room for stairs, look for a closet you can cut down, tuck a spiral staircase into a corner, or add a dormer (see page 61). Where you place stairs depends on how much headroom you have.
• Ask an architect or building contractor to check the floors for strength and movement. If they give much, double up each joist, especially where joists run for long distances or support heavy objects.
• If you have a forced-air heating system, heat the attic by extending runs from the level below or install an auxiliary unit. You also may need to reinsulate, as explained on page 44.

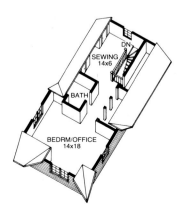

ADDING IN

BY REMODELING YOUR BASEMENT

"Look out below" may be just the advice to heed. From a remodeler's viewpoint, basements have certain built-in advantages. Heating, wiring, and plumbing are usually in place, in an area often roomy enough to create a whole new floor of living space. As a rule, interior stairways provide easy access, and if you're searching for a bargain-basement deal, you can probably do much of the work yourself. Nevertheless, a few problems may undermine even the best of plans. In many basements, water is an unwelcome guest, ceilings are too close for comfort, and natural light is nowhere to be found. There are solutions, however—if you're willing to work at them.

If you're planning to remodel a basement, keep the following tips at the top of your list.

• *Check for moisture.* You can cure condensation by building a new, insulated inner wall. Two coats of waterproof masonry paint will often stop water from seeping through the wall itself. To plug small leaks, force waterproof hydraulic cement into them and seal with masonry paint. If a damp concrete floor is a problem, fasten down strips, cover them with a polyethylene vapor barrier, and top with sub- and finish flooring.

• *Check the ceiling height.* You may want to cover up heating ducts, pipes, and other unsightly fixtures, if you have enough headroom. Measure from the floor to the bottom of the joists. Subtract a few inches for floor and ceiling materials, and you have the ceiling's highest point. Then, note the fixtures that drop below the joists; they'll set the ceiling's lowest level. If big portions of your basement are less than 7 feet high, your basement is not a good candidate for adding in.

• *How's the light?* Most basements are chronically dark. The usual solution is to brighten the scene with incandescent or fluorescent lighting, often sold in tandem with acoustic ceiling materials. Better yet, excavate to bring in natural light and access to the outdoors. Check the photograph *opposite,* and you can see how just a little digging created a walk-out patio. Inside, *upper and lower right,* artificial lighting, an opened-up stairway, and a width-doubling mirror wall, further help dispel any down-in-the-basement gloom.

ADDING IN

BY ENCLOSING YOUR PORCH

Finishing off a porch is an eminently sensible way to add more room to your house. It's not a difficult job for a skilled handyman, nor is it a budget-busting project, even if a professional does most of the work. Keep in mind, though, that the area must be structurally sound to start with. Without a solid foundation or sturdy roof supports, no porch can pass the rigorous test of daily living. One piece of advice before you begin: Try to keep everything on a 4-foot module. Building materials are based on this measure, which makes them easier and less expensive to install.

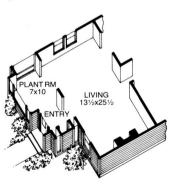

PLANT RM
7x10

LIVING
13½x25½

ENTRY

The quarry-tile-floored, plant-filled living room alcove *at right* was once a front porch. Converted, it adds floor space, an entry, and much-needed light to the living room.

If you'd like to turn a porch to equally good use, keep a few pointers in mind.

• If the existing floor is concrete, you're in luck; it's probably thick enough and strong enough to withstand the extra weight of new sidewalls. On the other hand, you may have to remove a floor made of patio block, brick, flagstone, or elevated wood and put in a new one with footings and proper reinforcing. Sturdy support is crucial if you decide to move heavy furniture or appliances into the room. In any case, make sure to insulate beneath the subfloor.

• Wooden or metal columns, posts, and ornamental iron are common materials for holding up the roof. When you're closing in a porch, try to incorporate these supports into the walls. If that's not possible, brace the roof at each bearing point, using double 2x4s or 4x4 posts, and remove the existing supports one by one. Then, as you would with any building project, frame in the new stud walls with 2x4s on 16-inch centers attached to headers and sill plates.

• Most porches have open ceilings. Plan to insulate between rafters and cover with drywall, ceiling tile, or another finish material. If you have to build a new ceiling over the porch, do one of two things: Support the rafters adjoining the house with joist hangers nailed to the house sheathing or to a ledger strip. Or, if you can, rest the rafters on a ledger strip.

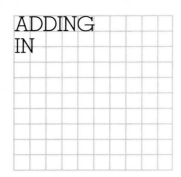

ADDING IN

BY ANNEXING YOUR GARAGE

Is the search for new living space driving you up a wall? Put on the brakes and take a look at your garage. If it's attached, the most expensive parts of any addition are already there: footings, a roof, and several exterior walls. If it's like most garages, it's probably close to a well-traveled room in the house—your kitchen, perhaps. At the same time, the whole thing is likely to be aboveground, so there's plenty of natural light, and chances are its design matches your home's exterior.

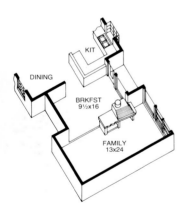

DINING

KIT

BRKFST
9½x16

FAMILY
13x24

Sold on the idea of giving your garage a change of space? Before starting, answer these questions:

• Is it structurally sound? If not, adding a new room may be less expensive than converting the garage.

• How will the change affect your home's floor plan? Will you be able to get in and out of the remodeled area easily?

• Can you tie in your present heating and electrical systems? (An independent source of heat may be an economical alternative.) Will new plumbing be a drain on your budget?

• Where will you put your car? Converting just a part of the garage is one solution; building a carport is another.

• Will local building codes or zoning ordinances interfere with the plans?

If the answers are encouraging, contact an architect or contractor. Professional advice will help get the project moving in the right direction, even if you plan to handle most of the design and building on your own. With the exception of installing mechanical systems, converting a garage is simple for a do-it-yourselfer.

Working example

Originally a 13x24-foot garage, the family room *at left* is a picture-perfect remodeling job. To provide a clear view of the backyard, the owners replaced the old entrance with operable awning windows and a large pane of fixed glass, *above*. A new back door, approached by a brick landing and sheltered by a roof overhang, leads to a breakfast room adjacent to the new family room.

The owners opened up the garage to the rest of the house by removing the wall separating the two spaces *at left.* The difference in floor height marks the spot. (If you plan a similar tactic, check with a contractor first.) In addition, the homeowners easily insulated the ceiling and outer walls and covered them with drywall.

BY REMOVING WALLS

Even in the tiniest houses, it's possible to make room for new and improved living areas. Think about your walls for a moment. Rather than enhancing the layout of your house, they may, in fact, be closing it in, their rigid dimensions creating a lot of little spaces where you really want two or three larger ones. If so, think about removing all or part of an interior wall. It's hard work—no doubt about that—but the change of space may open up possibilities you never thought of before.

By taking out an interior wall, you can alter the looks of your house dramatically. Two small rooms become one big room. An under-used hideaway becomes part of an inviting new family room. And the more walls that come tumbling down, the more you can divide space to your liking.

You don't have to remove a wall entirely to get the effect you want. Sometimes, just eliminating a portion of it will give you a view of an adjacent room, create a more open feeling, and add light to the area. In the house shown *at right*, for example, the owners removed walls to join the former living room, dining area, and kitchen for a contemporary, highly livable open plan. The mirrored wall of the dining area lengthens and widens the entire space. An arched cutout in the other wall gracefully connects the dining area to the kitchen.

Wall wherewithal

With a wrecking bar, you can whack out a normal nonbearing wall in just a few hours. The really tough part comes later, when you have to wheel out several hundred pounds of debris—and then patch in around the perimeter of the remaining walls and ceiling.

Before getting your whacks in, however, make *absolutely* sure the wall you're about to remove is indeed a nonbearing one, supporting nothing but itself. Nonbearing walls, or partitions, usually run *parallel* to joists and rafters. Bearing walls, which help hold up the house, run *perpendicular* to these members. Tampering with them could bring you and your house down to earth quickly. If you have any doubts at all, consult an architect or builder.

Also, before you start, determine whether the wall has any wiring, plumbing, or heating lines running through it. You can relocate them later; just make sure to shut off the systems in advance.

Be warned that knocking out a wall is likely to produce the biggest mess you've ever seen. Remove all furniture, or cover everything within range with tarps or plastic. Prepare yourself, too: Wear goggles, a hard hat, and, for additional protection, a face mask.

When the partition is down and out, you'll have to patch the walls and ceiling. At the same time, you'll also need to make a decision about the floor. Wood flooring that runs parallel to the former wall can be replaced without too much fuss. If it runs in the other direction, however, consider tiling or carpeting.

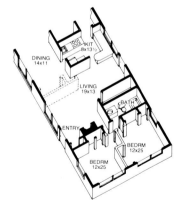

ADDING IN

BY REMOVING CEILINGS

You own a small house, and you're using every square inch from basement to attic. It works well enough, but somehow everything seems so *tight*. If you can't add on, don't give up. In fact, set your sights a little higher. By removing all or part of a ceiling, you can create wide-open spaces that make your home seem bigger than it is. You may lose a bit of attic storage/sleep space, but, as the photographs on these pages show, you're likely to bring sunshine to the rooms below.

Removing a ceiling takes some careful planning before you tear into it with hammer and crowbar. First, be sure your work won't damage or eliminate important structural members. If you plan to remove any joists, beams, or trusses, consult an architect or contractor. Here double 2x10s line an elegant 8x10-foot octagonal opening, with extra supports hidden behind them to strengthen the floor above.

Obviously, removing a ceiling means knocking out the floor of the attic or room above. Doing so often exposes part of the chimney, plumbing vents, and electrical wiring (shut off the power before you start). As you're planning, think about how you're going to reroute or cover up these elements.

At the same time, don't forget insulation. If you're opening a room below the attic, you'll have to take out the insulation in your attic floor. Make sure to replace it with new material—either polystyrene boards under drywall between rafters, or batts of insulation if you intend to install drywall over the rafters. Don't discard the existing insulation. Before ripping into the ceiling, gather it up in bags and store it for later use.

Like removing walls, taking away ceilings is dirty business. You'll produce a blizzard of dust, so either remove all the furniture or cover everything, including the floor, with tarps or plastic. Protect yourself, as well—wear goggles and a hard hat while you work.

If an attic loft is in your plans, you'll have to devise a new stairway. A wall-mounted ladder usually works best. You also may need a ventilating fan in the gable end to exhaust hot air.

1st FLOOR   **2nd FLOOR**

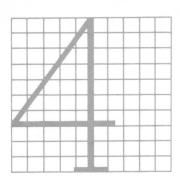

A PORTFOLIO
OF ADDITION
ALTERNATIVES

If you're convinced that nothing less than more square feet will solve your home's space problems, start imagining your ideal new addition. Where should the space go? What purposes will it serve? How much can you afford to spend? These and other considerations will start to shape your dream space into a realistic addition plan. This chapter shows how ten families found solutions to their space problems. One—or elements of several— could be the starting point for making more room at your house.

A FAMILY ROOM

The owners of the light-filled family room addition *at right* wanted a place formal enough for adult entertaining, yet easygoing enough for everyday family activities. This two-story space, built where a porch once opened out from their turn-of-the-century house, meets both criteria admirably.

Though the porch was demolished, several of its components survive—most notably those beams that crisscross overhead. Dramatic new double-decker windows open to ventilate the family room and balcony above (see plan).

The antique walnut mantel came from an architectural salvage firm. It tops off a new fireplace that was purchased to fit the space and surrounded by painted Dutch tiles.

Modern convenience blends with country charm in the stereo cabinet—a refurbished oak ice box that conceals state-of-the-art components.

Furnished with a table and a pair of Windsor chairs, a secluded niche beside the circular stairway (see plan) accommodates casual dining, children's projects, and table games.

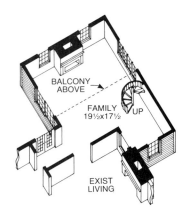

BALCONY ABOVE

FAMILY 19½x17½ UP

EXIST LIVING

AN EAT-IN KITCHEN

Ideally, a kitchen should have enough room for both working and eating. If your kitchen doesn't, adding to it may be one of your priorities. Keeping major fixtures and appliances where they are and simply adding eating space is a relatively economical solution. If, however, the work space in your kitchen is too limited, or if everything about it seems wrong, an addition gives you an opportunity—albeit a more expensive one—to completely restructure the way it works.

The goal of the kitchen addition shown here was to create a gathering place—in the owner's words, a "true heart of the home." For this family, that meant adding a light-filled dining area and giving the original pleasant, but small, kitchen a face-lift.

Preserving and even enhancing the character of this original 1900s shingle-style house was as important to the owners as gaining a new eating area. The addition's exterior shown *above* blends well with the rest of the house. Arched windows repeat the shape of windows at the front of the house, and the new gabled roof matches the pitch of the original.

Work on this 14x14-foot addition began with removal of an old "wash porch" at the rear of the house. The porch's sagging floor and crumbling understructure left the owners with little choice but to begin anew. They excavated into an adjacent hillside in order to lay a foundation that matched the level of the house. This made for a smooth transition between the old kitchen and new eating area—an important consideration in planning a kitchen addition.

The addition is separated from the original kitchen by a counter, shown on the plan *at right* and in the foreground *opposite*. The counter previously backed up to an exterior wall; that wall was removed and replaced by a new raised snack bar on the eating area side. In the original kitchen, the family opted for few changes, but did install new oak cabinets. The drop-in range was the only appliance they replaced.

More than a place to eat

If, besides lacking an eating area, your kitchen has awkward or inadequate work space, ask yourself why. Do you need more counter or storage space? New or better-placed appliances? Are light and ventilation sufficient? Adding on could give you an opportunity to make your kitchen work the way you've always wanted it to. If you plan to redesign most or all of a kitchen, keep these points in mind:

• Where are existing plumbing lines and would they have to be relocated? Generally, you can move a sink a few feet in any direction without getting involved in costly plumbing work; move it more than that and you'll have to extend branch lines from the original drainage stack.

• Do you want to relocate the range? Compared to water pipes, gas lines are relatively easy to relocate, but you may have difficulty venting a hood from some spots.

• Where will the refrigerator go? A refrigerator requires only a single 120-volt electrical receptacle (preferably on its own circuit). But the size of a refrigerator, coupled with the fact that it's your most frequently used appliance, demands that you plan a convenient location that accommodates its bulk.

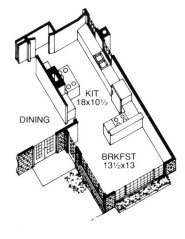

DINING

KIT
18x10½

BRKFST
13½x13

A MASTER SUITE

If your "master" bedroom seems more like servants' quarters, a bedroom addition could turn things around. Whether you simply add space to your present bedroom or go ahead and build a whole new one, generous new dimensions can help you fashion a masterful suite. Well-planned storage is a basic ingredient; comfortable seating is nice, too; and you may want to go further and include special features, such as a fireplace, study, or electronic entertainment center.

After enduring small closets and tight living space for years, the owners of the home shown here decided to expand their bedroom. To do so, they took advantage of a sound structure outside their old bedroom windows—the roof of a screened porch. With an architect and an interior designer, they devised a custom remodeling that fitted their needs exactly.

The new master suite was created by knocking out the bedroom end wall and enclosing the space over the porch. Extending the existing bedroom over the porch saved the expense of a new foundation and preserved the home's architectural style.

Outside, *above,* the house looks as though it hasn't changed in decades. To maintain continuity between the addition and the rest of the house, two old bedroom windows were saved and reset in the new end wall. Identical new windows, added to the front and back walls, balance the exterior and bring light into the new room.

Look out below

If you're planning to add on and are lucky enough to have a first-floor roof to use as a foundation, remember these structural facts:
• Few porches are sturdy enough to carry added weight. Have an architect or contractor assess the strength of your porch's roof, sides, and foundation. The roof and sides may need to be reinforced.
• The foundation may need only jacking and strengthening, or you may have to lay a new on-grade foundation and floor. An existing concrete porch floor probably can handle the extra weight.

Sleeping, seating, and storage

The new sleeping area shown *opposite* is in the space over the porch. Check the plan *below* and you'll see that the former bedroom has been divided into a sitting room, a dressing area, and built-in storage.

With the bed out of the way, the owners were able to install double clothes closets with built-in drawers, a floor-to-ceiling divider with book shelves and mirrors, and other specialized storage.

Abundant storage helps a bedroom live bigger. If you're thinking about adding or expanding a bedroom, consider adding closets, too. Once new space has been opened up, you can economically create closets with framing, drywall, and inexpensive doors. As you plan closets, keep these guidelines in mind.
• A deeper closet doesn't necessarily provide more usable storage space, since you'll need to leave room for access to the back.
• Allow a minimum width of 48 inches of rod space for each adult.
• If closet space is tight, consider outfitting part of it with double-tier rods at 3- and 6-foot heights. In the remaining space, a single rod, 6 feet high, will accommodate even long robes. Plan a height of 4 feet for children under 12 years of age.
• Closet shelves should be at least 12 inches deep to handle bulky items.

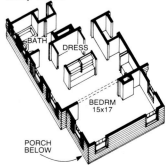

A CHILD'S ROOM

As your family grows and your children's interests change, your house often needs to grow or change, too. Children's ages help determine where to add on and what kind of space to add. A room for a new baby is going to be a child's room for a long time to come and is most conveniently located near the other bedrooms. On the other hand, a room added to meet the changing needs of an adolescent may serve that purpose for only a few years before it's turned into a guest room, den, or hobby room. For a teen, you might prefer to add a more versatile room, possibly one located outside the mainstream of family traffic.

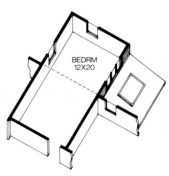

BEDRM
12X20

The owners of the compact Victorian house shown here needed a lot more space—a bigger bedroom for their teenage son, and a larger, updated kitchen.

Because the house was on a narrow lot with little room to grow, the new space was achieved by adding up two stories—and out only 10 feet. The addition, designed to complement the complex roof line and architectural style of the original house, is a successful blend of old and new.

The addition's lower levels consist of a new back entry and eating area, with a full basement underneath. Above, the teenager's second-story room—formerly 10x12 feet—grew to a spacious 12x20 feet. As the photo *opposite* shows, it comfortably accommodates his diverse interests.

Equally important, angular lines and clean, dramatic window styling give the room a grown-up look. And, when the boy leaves home, this space will lend itself just as well to other uses as a guest room or den, with an area reserved for him on return visits.

Room at the top

Prior to adding on, the bedroom ended at the beam in the top foreground of the picture *opposite.* In the new space, the architect reached up with a cathedral ceiling that follows the roof line. It not only changes the character of the room but provides more usable space. Large casement windows on all sides of the addition provide excellent ventilation, and a double-glazed, fixed window in the peak adds to the already abundant light.

Both the roof and sidewalls are fully insulated to ensure maximum comfort year round. To emphasize the dramatic lines and provide greater flexibility in redecorating when its main function changes, the room is finished in drywall and painted a versatile, go-with-anything white.

The new space's dimensions and angular lines suggested a theme for the room's furnishings, which capitalize on vertical space. Both the bunk beds and the shelving are tubular steel units that can be ordered in custom dimensions. The top bed, reached by ladder, is ideal for reading and games. At 20 inches above normal bunk-bed height, it has a treetop view of the neighborhood. Equipped with a railing for safety, it's also ideal for overnight guests. To avoid the awkward process of making up a formal bed at that elevation, guests use sleeping bags.

For smaller guests, consider lowering the upper bed to normal bunk-bed height. If two children will be sharing the new room, using standard-size bunk beds would let you designate one part of the room as sleeping/quiet-time space and the other for more active pursuits. Another alternative, if you're planning an addition for two children, is to design a space that lends itself to equal division, with similar allocations of windows, closets, and electrical outlets.

A FAMILY ROOM AND MORE

If you're planning to build an addition, create a design that will allow you to get as much use from the new area as possible. These two pages show a combination family room/dining room that does both its jobs beautifully. (Another space-efficient option might be a family room that converts to a guest room or a bedroom that incorporates specialized hobby space.) This addition also solves another problem that might be vexing you: how to gain ground-level access on a rear-sloping lot.

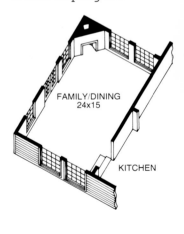

FAMILY/DINING
24x15

KITCHEN

The two "rooms" shown here—a conversation area *opposite* and a dining room *above*—are part of the same versatile, 24x15-foot space—a family room addition to a 75-year-old suburban house. Because the home's kitchen has no eating area, incorporating a dining space into the family room was part of the plan from the start.

The room's two sections are unified by a cheerful American countryside decorating scheme, white-painted walls throughout, and blue-trimmed windows on three sides. Two skylights—one directly over the coffee table and the other over the French doors leading to

the backyard—brighten the entire space. A warm-tone, easy-care quarry tile floor is another unifying feature that sets off the furnishings and patterned rugs.

Not only does the quarry tile look handsome, it also helps conserve energy. In winter, sun streaming though the tall windows warms the tiles. Acting as thermal mass, they retain heat for several hours and radiate it back into the room during the evening. (Simple roll-up shades block hot summer sun.)

Another plus: Quarry tile can be applied directly over a concrete floor. Since many other types of flooring require a vapor barrier and subfloor, using quarry tile in this addition saved a construction step.

(For more about flooring for your addition, see pages 154 and 155.)

Supplementing the heat-retaining effect of the quarry tile floor, perimeter baseboard units tie into the central heating system. A prefabricated heat-circulating fireplace provides warmth on chilly evenings.

Building at ground level
Because one of the owners' goals in building this addition was to gain eating space, proximity and access to the kitchen were important. The kitchen, however, was 10 feet above ground level. Bringing the addition up to house level with traditional concrete block foundation walls would have been expensive and could have resulted in a massive, unattractive foundation incompatible with the original exterior. Just as important, the owners wanted both a view of and access to their tree- and flower-filled yard. (For more about where to locate an addition, see pages 98-107.) To solve this problem, the owners built stairs from the new family/dining room and turned them into a welcoming asset. The view from the top is dramatic, thanks to a 3x5-foot birch balcony located at an arched opening that was formerly a window in the original kitchen wall. (Both of our photos were taken from this overlook.)

If this is the situation at your house, you might choose to build at ground level, as these owners did. Not only would you save money on foundation work, but you could gain a taller space under your existing roof line.

STRETCH
A WING

Several of the additions shown on the previous pages show what you can achieve if you add an entire new wing to your house. But what if you already have a wing, and building another isn't feasible? Maybe the answer lies with stretching the one that's there. Sometimes just a modest amount of new space, plus a lot more light, can make a big difference. Here's a case in point.

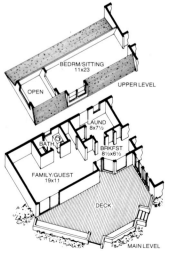

BEDRM/SITTING
11x23

OPEN   UPPER LEVEL

LAUND
8x7½

BATH

BRKFST
8½x6½

FAMILY/GUEST
19x11

DECK

MAIN LEVEL

The original wing on this Dutch Colonial home included a TV/guest room, bath, laundry, and breakfast room—all in just 11x17 feet. Extending the wing with an 8x11-foot two-story-high addition turned the TV room into a full-fledged family room, brought light into previously dim spaces, and granted easy access to a new deck outside. A new bay window (see plan) enlarges the original breakfast nook enough to make it comfortable for the family of four and makes room for a convenient passageway into the new family room.

Continuing the original roof line integrated the design of the extended wing with the original house and put it in harmony with the overall appearance of the neighborhood.

Fifty-foot-tall trees on the lot were another factor in deciding how and where to build. The owners were anxious not to damage either roots or limbs, and limited the wing's height and dimensions accordingly.

Incorporated into the space between the new wing and the house, the deck is accessible via sliding glass doors in the family room, a swinging door in the breakfast room, and

French doors from the original dining room.

Inside views

The exterior curve of the new roof shapes the interior as shown *at left,* adding visual interest and giving the illusion of more space than the extended wing actually has. A large, semicircular clerestory window in the gable end lets in lots of light and adds an unexpected note to the traditional design. Under the window, wall-to-wall built-in shelves hold books, pictures, and stereo speakers.

The difference in ceiling heights between the new and original parts of the family room creates drama, with a strong vertical emphasis. Light streams through the large window and benefits not only the family room, but the second story of the original house.

Upstairs, *opposite,* a bedroom overlooks the family room through a semicircular fixed-glass interior window. This window, which repeats the shape of the oversize clerestory in the addition's gable end, can be screened with a colorful, bottoms-up sailcloth shade. When the shade is open, borrowed light from the exterior window makes the bedroom seem brighter and more spacious.

A BUMP-OUT

Even a small addition can make a big impact on living space. Adding just a few feet could make room for anything from a walk-in closet in your bedroom to a breakfast nook in the kitchen to a hobby center in the family room. Bumping out expands your home's perimeter, often without the expense of a new foundation or roof, and usually without modifying plumbing, heating, and electrical systems. Re-angling exterior walls and moving one inside wall transformed a too-small bedroom into the contemporary master suite shown here on these pages.

Three-foot-deep overhangs and a sturdy deck supplied the roof and floor for this angular bedroom bump-out. The original 11x14-foot space, cut up by windows and doors, left room for little more than a double bed. Closet and storage space were inadequate, and the adjoining bath had no room for a tub.

By pushing a wall out to the edge of the overhang (see plan), the owners gained 184 square feet. This new space, plus some interior reshuffling, expanded the small bedroom and bath into a master suite.

Building out onto a section of wood deck that ran along the rear of the house eliminated the need (and cost) for any new understructure to support the project. A glass door at one end of the bump-out *below* provides access from the suite to the still-ample deck.

Beyond the bedroom, a 6-foot section of outside wall was bumped out 2 feet, shown at the bottom of our plan, enlarging the bath to accommodate a tub and double vanity. Because a tub—especially one filled with water—is heavy and requires plumbing connections, the owners set this portion of the addition on an entirely new foundation. The revamped bathroom includes a skylight and new windows.

Inside moves

Once the exterior bedroom wall was pushed out, the homeowners began work on shifting interior space. They expanded the bedroom to its present 15x17 feet by moving the wall on the bath side of the bedroom back 2 feet. To gain storage space, the existing bedroom closet was enlarged by merging it with a hall closet. To create another walk-in closet, they closed in the area once occupied by a built-in desk and combined it with borrowed space from a closet on the bath wall.

Shifting walls and reorganizing space created some projections and indentations *opposite,* which now house built-in shelves for books and collectibles, TV, and stereo. As a final special extra, a new fireplace warms the new suite.

A fixed-glass clerestory and smaller flanking casements, as well as the glass door, allow plenty of light into the room.

Structural considerations

If you don't have a deck to base your bump-out on, cantilever by extending floor joists or hang the structure from the eaves. Both methods cost less than building a full foundation. You also can purchase prefabricated, greenhouse-style bump-outs that you simply attach to the exterior wall around an existing window.

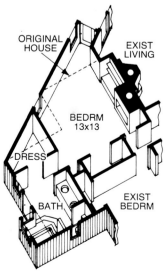

ORIGINAL HOUSE

EXIST LIVING

BEDRM 13x13

DRESS

BATH

EXIST BEDRM

A BAY

If you have a room that's small, dark, or lackluster, consider brightening its outlook with a new bay. Think of a bay as a shallow, windowed bump-out—one that adds architectural distinction inside and out. If the room's traffic patterns and seating areas conflict with one another, a bay may provide the few extra feet you need to make everything work. Prefabricated bay units come in a variety of sizes, shapes, and styles. What's more, unless your home has solid masonry walls, opening a wall and installing a bay is only a moderately difficult project.

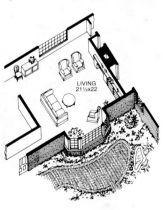

The bay window addition shown here replaced three small double-hung windows in the north wall of a once-dark living/dining room combination. The 17x35-foot room is in the middle of the home, and the owners found the area used more as a bridge between wings than as a comfortable place to relax. Traffic from the front door and other living areas formed a pattern that made arranging furniture difficult.

By bumping out the window wall to form a 3½-foot-deep bay, the owners were able to bring in more light and make the room more livable. As the photo *at right* shows, the bay also created a focal point around which to arrange seating. Instead of crisscrossing the room, traffic now skirts the seating group, which also offers views of the fireplace (at the left of the photo), as well as the new bay.

Because this home is built low to the ground, the bay is supported by a 4-foot-deep concrete frost footing topped with brick-faced blockwork. Many bays, however, can be cantilevered from existing joists. Because of its northern exposure and location in a cold climate, the bay's substructure was wrapped with a vapor barrier of 6-mil polyethylene sheeting and insulated with rigid urethane foam and batt insulation within the framing.

The original roof line was extended to cover the bay, as shown *above*. (A bay added to a taller house would have a distinct roof line of its own.) Prefabricated roofs are available in metal or wood, but this one was custom built. It was insulated and sheathed with 16-ounce standing-seam copper, which complements the cedar shake roof on the original house.

A DORMER

No space for an addition at the front, sides, or rear of your home? Maybe you can go up and out with a dormer. If so, you have two choices—shed and gable styles. A shed dormer, like the ones shown here, has a single sloping roof; a shed can run almost the entire length of a home's main ridge beam. A gable dormer, usually smaller than a shed, has two pitched roofs that meet at a ridge perpendicular to the main roof ridge. Choose the style that best serves your space needs and best harmonizes with the exterior appearance of your house.

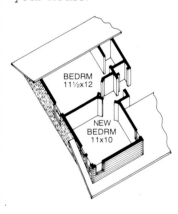

BEDRM
11½x12

NEW
BEDRM
11x10

Two bedrooms weren't quite enough for the young family that lives in this story-and-a-half house, but the boundaries of a small city lot precluded a ground-level addition. Their solution: Add *up*—in this case, with a pair of shed dormers that turned one of the existing upstairs rooms into two and the other into a commodious master suite.

The playroom shown *opposite* is a star attraction of one of the dormers. Imaginatively placed corner windows provide for maximum unbroken wall space within. And the new 10x11-foot room, now a place for a small child, will function equally well in the future as a bedroom, study, or guest quarters. Simple oak flooring and white drywall ceilings and walls assure versatility.

The second dormer (visible in the background of the photo *at right*) is the grownups' half of the expansion. It gives the owners a new master bath and dressing area, a more spacious sleeping space, and light from windows on all three sides of the dormer.

Examine the plan *at left* and the exterior view *at right* and you'll see that these dormers, which start at the ridgeline, are large in proportion to the original house. To minimize their mass and keep the house from looking top-heavy, the dormers were sided with cedar shingles, stained dark brown to blend in with the roof.

What about your house?

To comply with most local building codes, a dormer requires ceiling joists that are at least 7½ feet above the floor. The second floor of this home had plenty of existing head space, but many attics may not.

The roof slope of a shed dormer depends on the

amount of headroom needed at the outside wall and on the height of the ridge. To drain properly, the slope should be at least 2 to 2½ inches in 12 feet.

Because framing a dormer temporarily disrupts the supporting members of the roof structure, this part of the job should be done by a qualified professional. A moderately accomplished do-it-yourselfer could handle roofing, siding, and interior finishing.

Attic dormers

Building a dormer out from an unused attic is a little more complicated than from a second story because more framing has to be altered. In fact, if your roof is supported by trusses, you won't be able to add a dormer at all. But if you have rafters, and the ridge

beam is at least 10½ feet above the attic floor, your attic probably qualifies for a dormer addition. Here are a few other points to consider.
• Ceiling joists, or collar beams, may have to be raised to meet the 7½-foot minimum height, and you'll probably have to add more, since in most unfinished attics, collar beams are too widely spaced to properly support ceiling materials.
• Count on revamping an existing stairway or building a new one.
• Insulation must be installed for maximum heat and cold protection; for proper ventilation, cut a window in the gable end.

AN ENTRY

If your house has nothing but a door between the living room and the front step, don't despair. A more gracious, more gradual entry can be yours for the planning. And investing time and money makes sense for energy-conservation reasons as well as aesthetic ones. An air-lock entry, for example, can keep out chilly air in winter and warm air in summer. Whatever your motivation, adding an entryway to your front or back door can add both charm and comfort to your home.

Once distinguished by nothing more than a concrete stoop, the front of the New Orleans home shown here gained a sheltered downstairs porch, a sundeck above, and an air-lock entry. The owners needed relief from sticky summer heat and chilly winter rains. They also wanted to add character to their plain house so it would be compatible with more elaborate houses in the neighborhood.

Adding a porch across the front of the house was their first step. Weathered brick, set in a herringbone pattern, surfaces the porch, full-length steps, and walkway. The roof, supported by detailed, corniced posts, spans the porch and protects both the front door and front window. Up top, a decorative railing with matching posts continues the architectural style. The result: an addition that looks as if it's been part of the house all along.

After the porch was constructed, half of it was enclosed to create a spacious new air-lock entry that serves as an insulating space be-

tween indoors and out. With an air-lock entry you minimize drafts by closing one door before opening another. Besides conserving household energy, this new entry also provides people with a place where they can shed wet coats and boots.

The walls of the new entry shown *at right* are made of fixed glass covered with latticework of 1¼-inch pine lath. The glass panels make the vestibule inviting and attractive all year round, sealing out summer humidity and keeping winter rains at bay. The latticework offers shade in hot sunny weather and softly filtered light on dreary days.

The rest of the new entry reflects careful planning, too. Recessed ceiling fixtures provide night lighting but are unobtrusive during the day. A recycled cypress entry door furthers the addition's period look.

What does your entry need?
You may not require as extensive a plan as the one detailed here, or you may wish to do even more. But whatever you choose, reduce your energy costs by providing an air-lock buffer. All you need is enough space to fully close one door before you open the other.

A porch can supplement an entry by protecting against wind, rain, and harsh sunlight. As you can see here, a porch also can bring new charm to the front of your house.

To build either a porch or an entry, you'll probably need to lay a new on-grade floor or erect a perimeter foundation. Which you choose depends on how much elevation is re-

quired to reach the door of your home. For an entry or covered porch you won't need to pitch the floor for water drainage, but you'll still want to make sure it's smoothly finished or made of water-impervious material such as brick or concrete.

Consult with an architect or contractor if you have any doubts about structural considerations. An architect can also help you work out a style that will enhance your home's appearance.

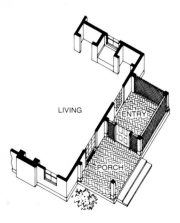

LIVING

ENTRY

PORCH

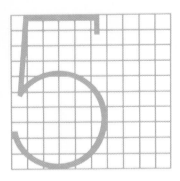

PLANNING YOUR ADDITION

The picture-perfect examples on the previous pages all add up to one thing: a good idea of what may work best for you. Now's the time to put your thoughts into action, and the only place to start, even for the simplest project, is with a plan—a precisely detailed design that takes into account the specific characteristics of your house and lot. This chapter discusses how to go about developing one; who can help out, if necessary; and what you can expect for your money. It also covers special topics, including strategies on conserving energy, using solar heat, and designing an addition for a disabled person.

DO YOU NEED A DESIGN PROFESSIONAL?

Well-conceived, well-designed, and well-built improvement projects will, in most instances, handsomely increase the price of your house when you decide to sell later on. Badly done work, however, not only will make your home a poorer place to live, it may actually diminish resale value—everything, in other words, you want to avoid.

That said, don't panic and immediately summon the most expensive architect in town to help with the plan. Fortunately, not every job is created equal.

Planning relatively simple tasks, like adding a dormer, bay, or bump-out; remodeling a kitchen or bathroom; or converting a porch or garage into living space, is an assignment you and a contractor, who may employ one or more designers to handle the details, can probably tackle together. Building these or similar projects isn't necessarily easy—in fact, it may be quite difficult—but solving the design and structural problems on paper usually isn't hard at all.

Help is on the way
For complicated interior changes, large additions, or perplexingly stubborn questions about appearance and function, professional assistance at the planning stage is often a good investment. Skilled help by itself won't add to the value of any single improvement, but it will, without a doubt, increase the chances of getting exactly what you want and may even allow you to save on unnecessarily costly labor and materials.

Who's qualified? Most architects and some house designers. If they're good, both architects and designers can perform one or more of the following services: bring your tentative ideas into focus, or suggest new, more effective ways of proceeding; prepare sketches to give you a rough idea of what the finished project will look like; develop final plans for a contractor or subcontractor to follow; and supervise the work as it goes along.

• *Architects.* An architect is probably the professional you think of first, and, often as not, he or she is a reliable choice (although some steadfastly refuse to do residential design). Of all the people concerned with some aspect of construction, the architect alone has the clearest conception of what it takes to add on, including a detailed understanding of building methods and materials. That knowledge is hard won. To set up shop as an architect, one must first complete a rigorous course of study at an accredited college or university, pass a state examination, and then spend a certain number of years apprenticing with a practicing professional. Only at this point can he or she get a license, put up a shingle, and go to work.

• *House designers.* This new class of professionals has only recently appeared on the home-improvement scene. Many are either interior designers who have begun working on exterior projects, or contractors who have a certain amount of experience in the field. Although some are very proficient at what they do and can match designs with architects, none has the architect's disciplined training or formal background. Even so, the difference between an outstanding designer and an outstanding architect is often the latter's expertise in engineering, which, for many kinds of home-improvement work, is not an essential qualification.

PLANNING YOUR ADDITION

WORKING WITH A DESIGN PROFESSIONAL

Realizing you need help is the first step toward a finished plan. Next on the agenda is finding the right person for the job.

Picking and paying

It's not a good idea to hunt hurriedly through the phone book, calling names at random. Instead, talk to friends, relatives, or neighbors who've worked with architects or designers in the past. Satisfied customers are always a pro's best reference. If you don't know anybody who has employed the kind of help you're after, check with local lenders, brokers, building inspectors, or the real estate editor of your town's newspaper.

Professional societies are another valuable source. Many design pros belong to either the American Institute of Architects (A.I.A. will follow their names) or, in the case of house designers, the American Institute of Building Designers. A call to the nearest chapter should yield several recommendations. During your search, always make sure that anyone you want to consider further is, in fact, interested in doing residential design.

When you've selected several candidates, set up an appointment with each, bring along photographs of your house, and chat in general terms about your ideas and what you hope to accomplish. (Don't worry about reaching into your pocketbook just yet; exploratory discussions are generally free of charge.) Share as much information as possible about your tastes, lifestyle, and your plans for the addition.

Ask to see representative examples of the person's work—accomplished professionals should have a portfolio of pictures to show you—and

solicit the names of previous clients. Later, pay a visit to one or more of them. Gauge their opinion of the work and see for yourself how well the new structure blends with the rest of the house.

Needless to say, money matters. From the outset, determine the amount you can afford to spend. Because most pros aren't bashful about going right up to the budgeted limit, be sure each person knows *exactly* how much you've allocated.

That figure, of course, will go a long way toward determining the services you'll get in return. Most architects and designers work at comparable rates, though experienced pros with lofty reputations may be more expensive than others.

For expert consultation—but no plans and no drawings—you'll almost always pay by the hour (anywhere from $25 to $125). For a series of increasingly detailed plans and specifications, you'll probably be charged either a flat sum or, again, an hourly fee.

If you want help every step of the way, a pro can do a complete set of drawings, obtain the required permits, help line up a contractor, buy building materials, and supervise the project from start to finish. For service like this, you'll ordinarily make installment payments equal to a percentage—often 15 to 20 percent—of the total construction costs, starting with an initial retainer and including certain out-of-pocket expenses incurred on the job (mileage to and from the site, for example).

When you've made your choice, it's time to get busy putting a plan on paper. As you'll discover, this is a painstakingly precise, but ultimately rewarding, experience.

(continued)

WORKING WITH A DESIGN PROFESSIONAL

(continued)

Let's assume you've hired someone for the duration, a practiced hand to guide the whole process of designing and building from start to finish. What happens, and how can you help?

The first thing to do is relax. After two or three weeks of careful searching, you should have the right person to transform your rough ideas into the intricately detailed drawings a contractor or subcontractors will need to put everything together. Believe it or not, one of the toughest parts of the job is now behind you.

Start the next phase with an amiable fact-finding mission. Invite the architect or designer into your home, show him or her around, and then sit down in a sociable setting to brainstorm about the changes you'd like to see. Take the opportunity to talk in more detail about your family's style of living and the ways in which you plan to use the addition.

You'll find that a good pro is like a well-trained discussion leader, drawing out your feelings and expectations, comparing them to the present layout of your house, and assessing what may or may not work in light of several factors: budget, local ordinances and codes, skilled labor in the area, and relevant design principles.

At this point, remember you're involved in a *conversation,* one that you're paying for. Don't stop talking—participate. You'll have no better chance to clarify your thoughts. Ask questions, explore alternatives, and don't automatically back away from your original thinking if, considering the advice you're given, it doesn't seem impractical.

You may need to get together again—or until all initial questions are satisfied, includ-

ing an acceptable timetable for the work. When that's done, the architect or designer, who now should have a fairly clear idea of the kind of addition you want, will usually snap several photographs of your house and lot to use in the early planning on paper.

Drawing it out

Over a period of weeks, the pro assembles a set of progressively more precise drawings that depict the addition and the way it fits into other parts of your house. These representations are, in effect, what you're *really* paying an architect or designer for. Frequently, however, homeowners are timid when it comes to evaluating plans and specifications—even though they'll have to shell out for the construction and live with the results.

Resist the inclination to accept whatever comes off the drawing board (unless, of course, it's just the design you're after). At each stage, make sure you understand both the general patterns and nuances of every drawing, asking—always—for probable costs and comparing them to your budget. Then, request alterations, if necessary.

• *Rough drawings.* Once a pro has arrived at an aesthetic decision, these are the easiest to execute—and to change. Sometimes called schematic drawings, they are basic, undetailed sketches showing the essential outline of the addition in relation to the rest of the house. Changes are simply made on tracing paper placed over the sketch.

• *Preliminary drawings.* They're more complicated than the name implies. At this point, the architect or designer may also begin bringing along materials samples for you to consider.

(continued)

WORKING WITH A DESIGN PROFESSIONAL

(continued)

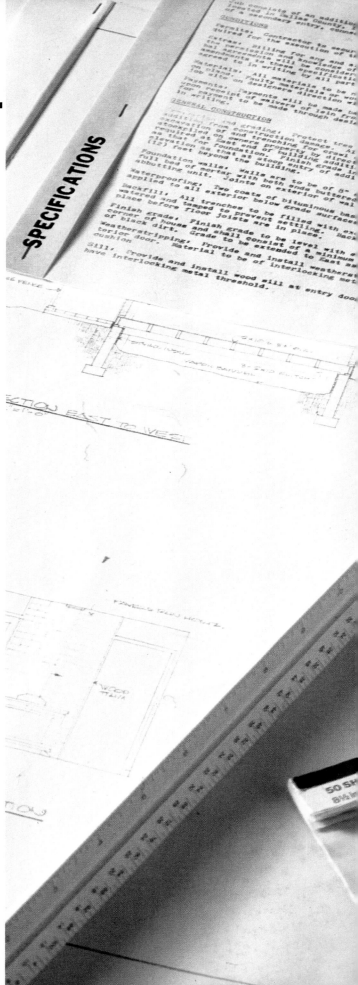

Preliminary drawings are done to the same size and scale as finished blueprints but don't contain as much technical detail and information. They often include three-dimensional renderings—models, really—of your house as it will look with the addition. The designer also may devise similar models of important interior spaces.

Keep your eyes and ears open; this is a critical stage in the design process. For the first time, you should be able to visualize clearly how the structure will look and work when the job is complete. Just as important, you'll also have a chance to make additional changes while they still can be done inexpensively on paper.

Now is also the time to begin firming up your budget. The preliminary drawings provide an accurate framework on which to pinpoint overall construction costs, including those for the basic shell, electrical and mechanical systems, and most finish work. By all means, listen to professional advice about building materials, and consider samples the architect or designer may show you. But don't hestitate to ask about less expensive, equally effective alternatives.

In any case, the object is to reach as many major decisions as possible, so you or the design pro or the contractor you'll hire has enough time to order materials before prices go up and make other selections if one or more items are unavailable. To save extra money, you may even want to take a few shortcuts on your own (see page 132).

• *Working drawings.* Also called blueprints, these are the last word on the subject— abundantly detailed instructions on where to build, how to build, and what to build with.

Blueprints come in a set, consisting of a site plan, foundation plan, and floor plans, in addition to elevation drawings, which indicate dimensions on vertical surfaces; one or more section drawings, showing interior views of solid structures; and several detail drawings that lay out special parts of the job.

Obviously, all working drawings contain precise dimensions. They also include lists, or *schedules,* of equipment and fixtures, and written directions, or *specifications,* covering building materials and methods to be used and the exact nature of the work to be done by the contractor or subcontractors.

All of this exact detailing serves as more than a construction guide. The information in the working drawings is also the raw data a contractor will evaluate before bidding on the project. And later on, it also will become an essential part of the legal agreement you sign with a builder (for more about contracts and contractors, see pages 138 and 139). Needless to say, major changes are ill-advised at this point, unless you have money to burn and time to waste. On the other hand, minor changes can be made right on the drawings.

Additional services

With a plan on paper, many homeowners take over and oversee the rest of the project themselves. However, the architect or designer can do other things for you: supervise the entire job; deal with contractors, suppliers, and building inspectors; and make sure the work proceeds on schedule according to the agreement (for a complete discussion of these and other practical matters, see Chapter 9).

CONSERVING ENERGY

Unless you're one of the lucky few who live where it's never too warm and never too cold, a good remodeling plan will be even better if it specifies features that keep energy in and utility bills down. Fortunately, architects, designers, and builders now recognize the value—for them and their clients—of tightening up residential projects without greatly increasing construction costs. Whether you're doing all or part of the job yourself or relying on hired help, many of the following basic suggestions should be part of the working drawings.

• *Insulation situation.* In most cases, you'll need to insulate every outside wall. Consider bundling up pipes and heating ducts as well, especially those running through non-living areas. You also may find it necessary to insulate parts of the house—basement, porch, attic, or garage—where you're thinking of ''adding in.''

• *Seals of approval.* Nearly one quarter of all energy leaks in existing homes occur along the soleplate, a board that rests atop the foundation walls and serves as a footing for first-floor wall studs. The specifications should include a method to plug this single long crack. (Plan to insulate the foundation wall itself with rigid styrene foam.)

You may be surprised to know that a costly amount of heated and cooled air can seep through electrical outlets on exterior walls. Adding inexpensive plastic gaskets to the materials list will solve the problem before it develops.

Specifications also should call for caulking at every construction joint, particularly where new lumber meets the original house. Surfaces that are merely nailed together are less effective barriers.

Plan to caulk all exterior doors, windows, and other openings with latex, acrylic, or silicone compounds. At the same time, specifying double-pane or even triple-pane windows is a good idea in many areas of the country. Make sure, too, that building instructions require each exterior door and window to be tightly weather-stripped.

• *Welcome breezes.* On the other hand, some work shouldn't be *too* tight. If, for example, your design calls for an insulated crawl space, it also must include vents that allow moisture to escape and prevent condensation from damaging the insulation. Similarly, if you're planning to transform an attic into living quarters, be sure to make gable and soffit vents part of the design. Combined, they stop heat from building up, usher cool outside air in, and protect insulation from excessive moisture. You may even want to install an attic fan to help boost the airflow.

• *Other tips.* Try placing closets on exterior walls: They'll serve as a buffer between indoor and outdoor environments. Popular cathedral ceilings are summertime delights because they allow warm air to rise well above head level. In winter, of course, this is a disadvantage; think about installing a ceiling fan to push the warmth gently back down. Finally, shrubbery planted near the foundation not only will shield the walls from winter winds, but also will provide shade and cooling evaporation during the summer.

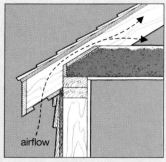

airflow

In most parts of the country, your plan should stipulate an adequate amount of insulation, not only for exterior walls, but for ceilings, as well. Your architect, designer, or contractor can give you sound advice on just how much you'll need and where.

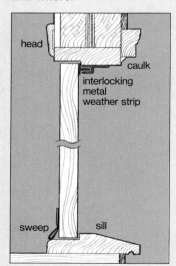

head

caulk

interlocking metal weather strip

sweep

sill

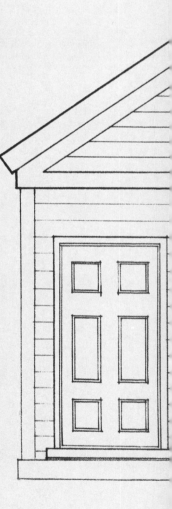

An exterior door that can stand up to the elements should be near the top of any materials list. If you choose one made of solid wood, you also may want to buy a storm door, especially in regions where winters are very cold. Fully insulated doors are another possibility. In any case, plan to install weather stripping around the entire doorway.

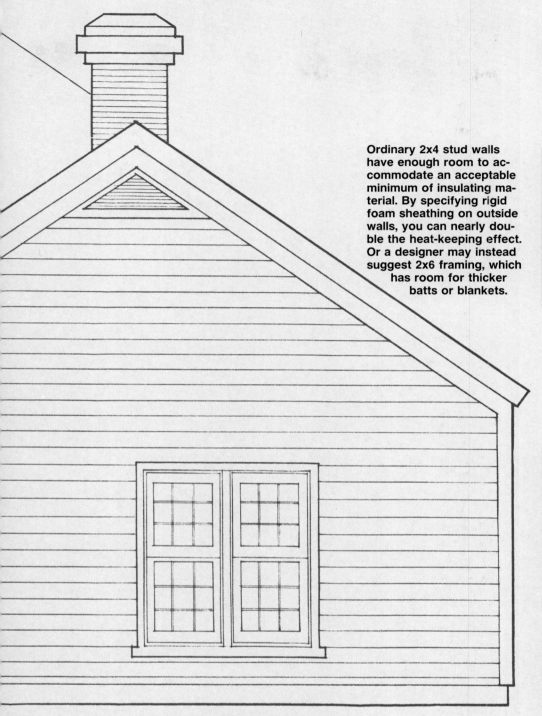

Ordinary 2x4 stud walls have enough room to accommodate an acceptable minimum of insulating material. By specifying rigid foam sheathing on outside walls, you can nearly double the heat-keeping effect. Or a designer may instead suggest 2x6 framing, which has room for thicker batts or blankets.

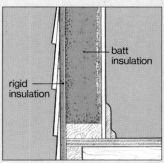

batt insulation

rigid insulation

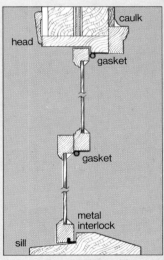

caulk

head

gasket

gasket

metal interlock

sill

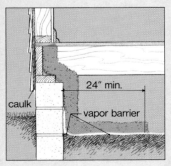

caulk

24" min.

vapor barrier

If the design specifies a crawl space instead of a basement, weatherproof it by positioning a vapor barrier, as shown at left, and then fitting fiber-glass insulation around the exterior walls. The insulation should extend at least 2 feet in from the walls. Also caulk the joint between siding and foundation.

Most plans include either double-hung or casement windows. The most energy-efficient kind have insulated glass panes. You can tighten them up further by installing weather stripping between the movable and stationary parts of each window. Caulking the window frames will form an even more solid seal.

COULD YOUR ADDITION TAP ENERGY FROM THE SUN?

Nowadays, enlightened plans often incorporate ways to use sunshine as an extra source of energy. Solar-heated bump-outs, enclosed porches, and remodeled garages are only three of the many likely designs that can easily be turned into *sunspaces,* rooms that are little more than tightly insulated areas with large south-facing windows.

Sunspaces not only provide the additional living space you're after and heat themselves in the process, they may even help to warm the rest of your house. Including passive solar features may boost initial construction costs a bit, but a well-designed sunspace will return that investment many times in the form of lower utility bills.

All good solar systems have three important characteristics: They collect, store, and control the sun's energy. Ordinary double- or triple-pane windows make excellent collectors. For best results, angle them to increase heat gain as much as possible.

Storing energy is no mystery, either. Masonry floors or tanks of liquid will absorb the warmth, hold it throughout the day, and then radiate heat back into living areas when the sun goes down.

Controls are equally simple—no knobs, dials, or unsightly mechanical wizardry. Doors and vents between the sunspace and other rooms will help move warm air where you need it most; insulation in the walls and over the glass at night will keep it there. Overhangs, awnings, and roll-down canvas shades are inexpensive devices that will hold heat in after sundown and hold it back if the day gets too hot.

Though a smoothly functioning sunspace is easy to de-

scribe, designing a similar system for any one house may be a tricky problem. Whether or not it's practical depends on where you live, where you plan to add on, the position of your house, and many other considerations, not the least of which is your budget.

It's usually wise to consult with an architect, designer, or builder who's done this kind of work in the past. He may, in fact, suggest a different type of passive or even active solar heating system that would fit in better with your plan. As you would under other circumstances, inspect previous jobs to find out just how effectively the sun is working for homeowners in your area.

Hot water
The active solar system shown *opposite, top* does a single task well: It helps heat this home's water supply. The roof-mounted panels collect energy from the sun and transfer it to water-filled tubes running between the panels and the heater. A small pump circulates the water.

A natural fit
The sun-drenched addition shown *opposite, center* is both a greenhouse and a pleasant dining area. Vents near the top allow excess heat to escape during the summer. During the winter, the home's brick sidewall absorbs warmth from the sunspace and releases it into other parts of the house.

A sunny side
In the sunspace shown *opposite, bottom,* angled glass panels collect heat to be stored in a rock bed floor topped with brick pavers. The shades at the top can be lowered to keep warm air in at night and, during the days, to keep overly strong sun out.

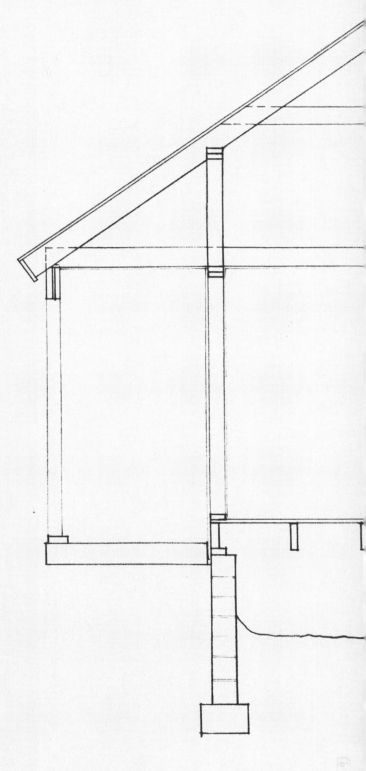

PLANNING FOR A DISABLED PERSON

For a disabled person, otherwise routine movements and activities are, to some degree, more difficult—perhaps even impossible—in an environment *not* adapted to his or her special needs. If a member of your family is disabled in some way, you probably have already modified the layout of your house to accommodate that person's specific requirements. Designing an addition may be only a matter of incorporating those features and changes that already have proved successful.

The following advice applies mostly to wheelchair-bound individuals, whose ways of coping with interior layouts ordinarily demand the most extensive design adaptations. At the same time, we can give you only a general idea of things you may need to consider. To arrive at a design that works best for your particular situation, consult with an architect or house designer who has some experience in developing plans for disabled persons.

• *Doors and windows.* Doorways and corridors must be wide enough so a wheelchair user can maneuver comfortably. Doors with double-action hinges are often the most convenient because they can be pushed open from either direction. Pocket, accordion, and bifold units are other acceptable alternatives to conventional swinging doors.

Horizontally sliding windows, casement windows, and awning windows usually are easier to operate from a sitting position than double-hung windows are. Obviously, all controls should be within reach.

• *Kitchens.* How you design a new kitchen depends primarily on how the disabled person

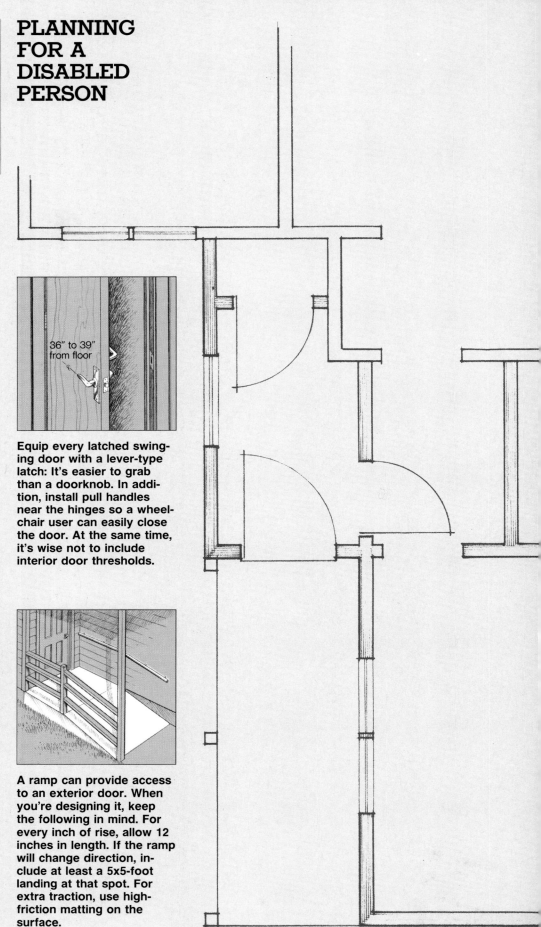

Equip every latched swinging door with a lever-type latch: It's easier to grab than a doorknob. In addition, install pull handles near the hinges so a wheelchair user can easily close the door. At the same time, it's wise not to include interior door thresholds.

36" to 39" from floor

A ramp can provide access to an exterior door. When you're designing it, keep the following in mind. For every inch of rise, allow 12 inches in length. If the ramp will change direction, include at least a 5x5-foot landing at that spot. For extra traction, use high-friction matting on the surface.

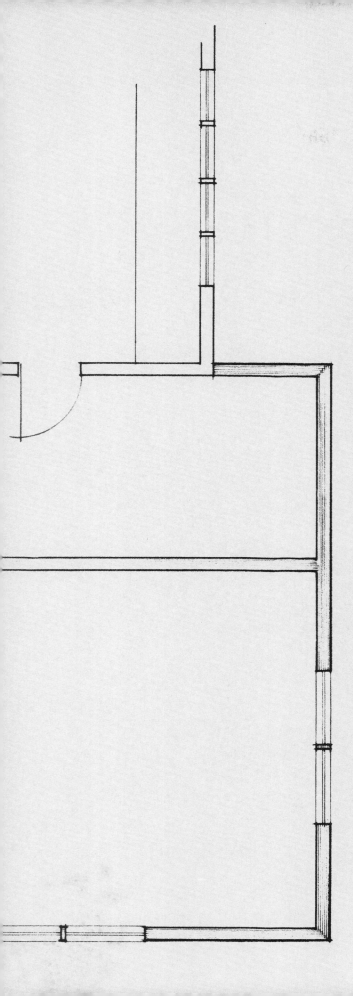

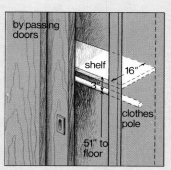

Open storage systems are convenient for everyone; where possible, consider stackable cubes, lightweight trays, or bins on casters. When you're positioning closet fittings, use the dimensions shown here as guidelines. If space permits, select pocket doors or draperies with pull cords to provide easier access.

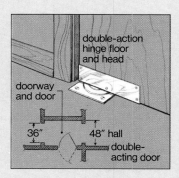

To make it possible for a disabled person to move easily from one room to another, plan all doorways to be a minimum of 36 inches wide. And if practical, design hallways that are 48 inches across. Double-action doors, like those sometimes used between kitchens and dining rooms, are easy for a wheelchair user to operate.

will use it. Enthusiastic cooks, who'll spend hours in this area, need plenty of room to move between sink, stove, and refrigerator, but not so much that they take up a lot of their time just maneuvering about. Access to appliances and storage is also vital. Well-developed standards exist for laying out a kitchen so wheelchair users can make their way around safely and comfortably. An experienced design pro will be able to help with all the details.

• *Baths*. Here convenience and safety are the important objectives. As with kitchens, a whole set of time-tested specifications, along with a wide range of adapted fixtures and fittings, will help guide the layout. Again, your architect or designer can give you valuable assistance. If you want to get an idea on your own of workable configurations and clearances, write to the Veterans Administration, Washington, DC 20420.

Helping the blind

Most blind persons adapt quickly to specific layouts, memorizing the routes they must take. However, when you're planning an addition a blind person will use, there are things you can do to help smooth the way.

• Avoid including unnecessary changes in level or structural projections.

• Don't plan steps and stairs with open risers or square nosings.

• Ask for building materials that reflect sound rather than absorb it.

• Change floor materials from one room to another, especially near potentially dangerous areas.

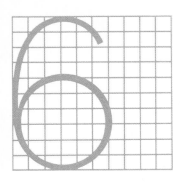

BUILDING
AN ADDITION

Earlier in this book, you learned how to evaluate your family's living area needs and weigh your remodeling and addition options through the process of planning an addition. This chapter documents the main construction stages in a typical adding-on project and tells what you can expect to happen during each. Of course, no two projects follow the same construction sequence in every detail, but just about all begin with excavation and foundation work, then proceed through framing and closing-in operations. After the shell has been completed, the exterior and interior are finished. Let's begin with looks—inside and out—at the new room you'll see take shape throughout the chapter.

THE END RESULT

The addition shown here solved several problems for the owners of a one-level ranch house. First, they wanted to correct a problem that resulted from a previous family room addition. It was adjacent to the garage and not handy to other main living areas.

The owners also wanted to expand and enliven their outdoor living area and gain a better view of the backyard.

Lastly, because the house sits on a corner lot, the owners felt a need for an entry from the side street.

Their architect's solution: a major, new one-room space off the rear of the house that integrates the existing family room, dining area, and kitchen, and incorporates a new entry.

The room's most prominent element, a vaulted cathedral ceiling with venting skylights, gives a feeling of spaciousness not possible with standard-height ceilings. Natural oak woodwork, light-colored walls, and beige carpeting further the light, airy look of the space.

The photograph *at right* shows the room from the hallway leading to it. To the left is a handy pass-through serving counter with custom cabinets beneath (not shown). The pass-through opening formerly was the kitchen window. Access to the kitchen is through the hallway and from the new living area. To the right are the family room, closet, and entry.

For before and after views of the exterior, turn the page.

(continued)

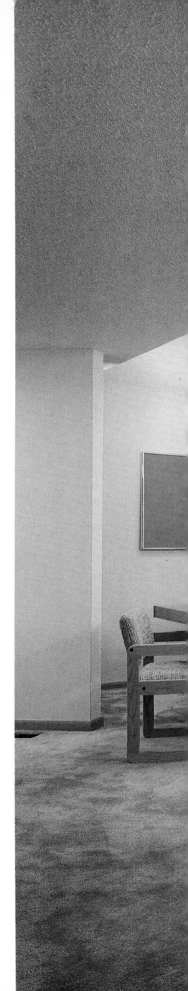

THE END
RESULT
(continued)

Check our view of the original rear exterior *opposite, top,* and you can see that the architect began with an L-shaped house. Hedges bounded a patio accessible from the kitchen—in the center of the house—and from the former family room addition at left.

Now examine the large photo. The new addition fills in part of the L and projects several feet beyond the former family room. The projection accommodates a new side-lighted entry, changing the home's orientation from one street that bounds the corner lot to the other (see floor plan *opposite, top right*). An angular deck wraps around from the entry to new outdoor living areas (at far right in our photo).

Big double windows at one corner of the addition and single windows at the other bring light and views not only to the new family room but to the kitchen as well.

Outside, the same brick veneer used on the existing structure visually ties the addition and original areas together. A new roofscape and matching shingles on both the new and existing roofs further blend the addition into the overall setting.

Take one more lingering look at the "before" view. It'll change dramatically on the pages that follow.

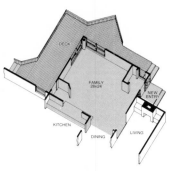

EXCAVATION AND FOUNDATION WORK

Prepare for a mess the day workers arrive to break ground for an addition. How big a mess they make depends largely on what sort of underpinnings the new room will have. If it will be built on piers or posts, excavation will consist of nothing more than digging a series of holes to below the frost line. Then concrete footings will be poured in the bottom of the holes. Wood posts or concrete piers atop these footings will support the addition. If your new room will be built on a foundation—as was the one shown here—your yard will suffer considerably more wear and tear. Here's what to expect.

On day one, the contractor will probably bring in a backhoe or other heavy equipment to dig trenches. Next will come a delivery of concrete blocks, lumber, and/or a truckload or more of ready-mix concrete.

After excavating, the contractor will pour footings, concrete pads on which the weight of the structure will rest. The foundation itself might be poured concrete, concrete blocks (the material used here), or even rot-resistant all-weather wood.

If you've decided on poured concrete, forms will be erected atop the footings; once the concrete has been placed and allowed to set, the forms will be stripped away. Concrete block walls, however, go up one block at a time. Treated wood foundation walls are constructed much the same as are the stud walls shown on the following pages.

1 Here's how the situation will look after the foundation has been completed. Notice that the top course of blocks covers only a portion of those in the course below. This provides a support ledge for the brick veneer that will face the addition. Brick has been removed from the original exterior walls that will be affected by the new room, as have fascia and soffit boards.

2 A tripled 2x10 center beam fits into a pocket in the house wall. Floor joists rest atop this beam and the foundation.

3 The other, outer end of the center beam fits into a similar pocket in the new foundation. Unless your plans call for a complicated floor system, carpenters probably can frame joist work and cover it with plywood subflooring in one day. At that point, your new room will resemble the big platform shown in our large photo.

1

2

3

1

2

3

4

FRAMING
THE
STRUCTURE

Now begins one of the most exciting phases in any construction project. To a symphony of power saws and hammers— scented by the aroma of fresh-cut lumber—you'll see your new room take shape. Framing crews work fast. Usually they lay out and assemble wall sections on the deck, then raise and nail them into position. Within a matter of hours, wall framing will be in place and temporarily braced with diagonals like the ones shown in our photos. Next, carpenters frame the roof—a more exacting, time-consuming job. In just a few days, the skeleton of your addition will be completed.

Framing work is often called "roughing." Since framing members will be covered inside and out, appearances don't matter. What *is* important is that everything be constructed plumb, level, and "true," with adequate strength and nailing points for sheathing and finish materials.

Typically, carpenters frame the walls and roof as indicated on the working drawings. Most plans still call for 2x4 walls spaced 16 inches from center to center (the method used in our example), but many architects now specify 2x6 stud walls on 24-inch centers. The additional 2 inches of wall thickness makes room for more insulation.

Attaching the addition to the existing structure poses special construction problems. To make the addition an integral part of the building it adjoins, the roof lines and the common walls must be tied together. The photo insets show how this was done in our example.
1 Here's an inside view of how the new and old roofs join. Each new rafter had to be individually cut to conform to the existing roof slope.
2 The new room will have a complex ceiling system that rises to the ridge in the center and drops to conventional ceiling height in the foreground and background.
3 By themselves, stud walls are rather flimsy. It takes ceiling joists and rafters to lock them together into a solid unit. Here joists were hung with metal hangers from a header nailed to existing rafters.
4 Rafters were notched to fit atop double 2x4 headers and secured with metal hangers.
5 Extra framing surrounding windows includes a header up top and a sill, like this one, below. Short studs below the sill are called *cripples*.

87

CLOSING IN

As carpenters complete the framing for an addition, they then cover it with *sheathing*—sheet goods that serve as a structure's underwear. Again, appearances aren't important; after the sheathing is covered with finish materials— roofing, siding, and interior drywall or paneling—you'll probably never see it again. Often windows and exterior doors are installed at this stage to "close in" the addition and protect it from weather.

Closing in not only completes a structure's shell, but also helps strengthen it. Modern-day framing and sheathing systems use relatively weak materials that tie together into one strong, cohesive whole. Framing, sheathing—even, to some extent, windows and doors— contribute to a building's strength.

Here the walls were sheathed with fiberboard and the roof with exterior-grade plywood. Fiberboard sheathing—compressed mineral fibers faced with layers of paper—is inexpensive, cuts with a knife, and offers some insulating value. If your addition's walls will be shingled, you'll need to sheath them with plywood; if you decide on plywood siding, you may not need sheathing at all. Roofs are almost invariably sheathed with plywood.

Sheathing work goes even faster than framing. Each 4x8-foot sheet covers a lot of wall or roof territory and requires a minimum of cutting and fitting. Even a complex roof like this one can be sheathed in a single day or less.

At this point, your contractor also may decide to install the windows and doors—especially if cold or wet weather might impede interior work. Once again you'll probably be surprised at how quickly your addition is coming along. Prefabricated windows and doors come off the truck as complete units—sashes, frames, hinges, and all. Workers need only fit them into the rough openings, plumb and level the units, and secure them with a few nails or screws.

Now your addition is beginning to look like something to live in, but be warned that the most tedious and time-consuming jobs lie ahead.

INTERIOR ROUGHING

Up to the time your addition is closed in, you'll be seeing one set of specialists at a time—excavators and masons for the foundation, carpenters for the framing and sheathing. Now you, your architect, or your contractor has to deal with several crews—and sometimes with them working at the same time. Electricians will rough in the wiring. A heating contractor will run pipes or ductwork. If your addition will include a new bath or kitchen, plumbers will install drain and supply lines for the fixtures. Carpenters will be around most of the time, completing framing details, adding insulation, and closing up the walls with drywall after the electrical, heating, and plumbing workers have completed the hidden parts of their systems.

As with rough framing, rough electrical, heating, and plumbing work deals with elements that go inside walls, under floors, and over ceilings. Precision and good workmanship are more important than what things look like.

Building codes come into play here, too. After systems have been roughed, but before the walls have been closed up, you'll probably be visited by a building inspector who will inspect the rough work and indicate approval by "signing off" the project. (The inspector may be back later, after finish materials and fixtures have been installed, for another look.)

The big photo here shows the scene that will greet the subcontractors as they arrive. Here's a synopsis of what each will do.

Wiring

An electrician's goal at this point will be to determine how to tap your new room into the existing system, install boxes for every light, switch, receptacle, and other electrical outlet your plans call for, and tie it all together with cables. He won't, however, install devices in the boxes or make final connections until drywall has been installed.

If yours is an older, underpowered home, you may need to have additional electrical service brought in. The electrician will then probably install a new, bigger breaker box that will serve the entire house. If your present electrical service has adequate reserve, the electrician may simply tap off it with a subpanel for the addition.

Heating and cooling

If your addition will be heated with electric baseboard units, an electrician will install outlets for these, too. But if your plans call for forced-air heating and/or cooling, you'll need the services of yet another tradesman. Again, whether you'll need a new furnace and cooling equipment or can merely extend existing duct runs depends mainly on the capacity of your present system.

Plumbing

Plumbers have a couple of jobs to perform at this stage. First, they rough in the drain-waste-vent lines that will service the various water users in your addition. Secondly, they tap into existing plumbing lines and run plastic or copper pipes to the locations where the fixtures will be. Here again, the plumbing lines make their way through the framing, and fixtures won't be installed until the finishing stage.

1 Regardless of whether a subcontractor is doing electrical, heating, or plumbing work, he must plan fixture installations that will take into account the thickness of finish materials such as drywall, plywood, or paneling. Here carpenters created a dropped soffit where electricians installed three canister lights.

2 One of the last things carpenters do before closing up walls and ceilings is install insulation. Here fiber-glass batts were fitted into the cavities between joists in the cathedral ceiling. For more about insulating an addition, see pages 72 and 73.

1

2

EXTERIOR FINISHING

Most exterior finishing jobs aren't as time-consuming as interior work, but their progress depends far more on weather conditions. Asphalt roofing shouldn't be installed when it's raining, very cold, or very hot. Masonry work also shouldn't be done at or near freezing temperatures. When timing is critical, your contractor may send crews to get started on mechanical and interior work before the roofers, carpenters, or masons arrive. Here's what to expect when they do show up.

Exterior finishing usually starts at the top. Compare the photo here with the one on pages 88 and 89, and you'll see that the rafters have been trimmed with fascia boards at the ends and soffits under the eaves. The roof sheathing has been covered with asphalt felt, and bundles of shingles await the roofers.

Once weather conditions are right, roofing goes fast. Roofers nail down shingles in overlapping courses, starting at the eaves and working up. Asphalt shingles, the type used here, have heat-activated seals on their undersides. Sunlight melts the seals and glues the shingles to each other, protecting against wind damage. (To learn about other roofing options, see pages 126-129.)

If you've chosen man-made or natural wood siding materials for the walls, carpenters will do the work. Plywood siding goes up almost as quickly as the sheathing did. Lap siding and shingles take more time. (See pages 110-121 for buymanship information about siding materials.)

Masonry work is the slowest of all. Mortar must be mixed, bricks or stones painstakingly fitted into place, and mortar joints smoothed to repel rain. Our inset photos show some points to look for.

1 Metal *ties* bond masonry veneer to the framing. Here the mason has nailed a tie to a stud, then "thrown" a line of mortar for the next course.

2 After the next course has been laid, the mason bends the tie down atop it, then throws another line of mortar.

3 Careful initial planning assures that the tops and bottoms of door and window openings will line up with mortar joints. Later, a masonry stoop will be installed here.

BUILDING
AN ADDITION

Here the walls and ceilings have been covered with drywall and the drywallers have taped the joints and filled the dimpled nail holes. Note, also, that fiberglass insulation has been fitted carefully around all windows to prevent the passage of air through this normally leaky area. Detail 1 shows this up close and also reveals the polyethylene film that forms an impermeable barrier against escaping vapor. The more tightly sealed this barrier is, the better. Detail 2 focuses in on an electrical switch. If the hole in the drywall panel was cut too large, the drywallers will fill the void with joint compound. In detail 3, the panels have already been nailed in place. Still to be done, though, is the taping of the joints between panels and over nail holes. Generally, this is a multi-step process.

1

2

3

INTERIOR FINISHING

Before interior spaces can be finished, they must be insulated. That includes surrounding the space with insulation between the rafters and/or ceiling joists, wall studs, and sometimes between floor joists, as well as packing it in the crevices between the framing members and the door and window frames. After this, a layer of polyethylene film must be fastened to the framing to prevent the passage of moisture out of the structure.

With these prerequisites out of the way, the drywalling or plastering crew can install the wall and ceiling surfaces. This process generally takes several days.

After the drywallers leave, a second layer of flooring goes down over the decking (except when thick tongue-and-groove floor decking has been used). Typically, particleboard is used in all areas other than those where hard surface or resilient flooring will be laid.

Next, painters cover the walls and ceilings with a primer, then a finish coat of paint. The finish carpenters follow, setting the interior doors and trimming out the addition with the types of moldings specified in the plan. After this is done, the painters return and clear-finish or paint doors, windows, and other woodwork.

Floor materials, except carpeting, usually are laid next. Then, plumbing, electrical, and heating/cooling crews return to finish up their installations. Plumbers set any remaining fixtures and make all water connections, and electricians hook up all wiring devices, hang fixtures, and energize the circuits. The heating/cooling people install thermostats and register grilles, and balance the system. Finally, if carpeting has been specified, carpet-layers install it.

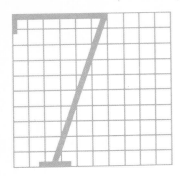

FITTING IN

Adding on to a home is no easy task. To fit in with its physical surroundings and with family life, a new addition needs careful planning. Its exterior design should complement both the existing house structure and the landscape. The interior must tie in efficiently with your household's mechanical systems, traffic patterns, furnishings, and habits. On these two pages, we show an addition that fits in so well it looks as though it's always been there. In the rest of this chapter, you'll find drawings, photos, and advice to help you make your own addition equally successful.

MAKING A MATCH

The house shown here is a textbook example of how to fit an addition—in this case a family room—into both an existing space and an established lifestyle.

The site of the family room was once an unheated open porch. Next to it was a rarely used jalousie-windowed Florida room.

By turning these pleasant but not fully functional spaces to the greatest possible advantage, the owners were able to create an "addition" without extending foundations or disrupting their home's architectural scheme.

The addition's exterior is a harmonious blend of new and old. The cedar shingles that replaced the old porch's fiberglass roof match those of the house; white siding and trim and a red brick chimney also harmonize with the original brick house. Tempered thermal glass panels in the new roof skylight a cathedral ceiling in the family room, completing the porch's transformation to an integral yet special part of the house.

The former Florida room's jalousie windows were replaced with a solid wall to make a cozy bar and game room (not shown). It opens to the family room, expanding space visually as well as actually.

The rearranged interior spaces make it possible for the owners to enjoy their "new" rooms year round. In warm weather, they can step directly from the family room to a patio. When the weather turns cold, the family enjoys a view of woods and hills. The interior temperature stays comfortable throughout the year, thanks to a heat pump mounted on a slab next to the base of the new chimney.

FITTING IN

WHERE'S THE BEST PLACE TO ADD ON?

Before you plan an addition for your house, you'll need a clear idea of what kind of addition will work and look best, and where it should go. The type of house you live in is the major factor here—different types of houses lend themselves to different types of additions. You'll probably find your house type on these two pages; if not, you're likely to find one or two others that will give you clues to the style and shape of addition that would best suit your house.

One person's raised ranch is another person's bi-level or split of some kind. Terms vary from region to region, and in fact the lines are not always absolute. To give you a clearer idea of what some basic house types are and what kinds of additions work well with them, here are brief descriptions of five major house types.

• *Ranch.* Usually a one-story, low-to-the-ground structure with wide overhangs. A *raised ranch* has its basement area partly aboveground, but stairs from outside usually lead directly to the main-level living area.

• *Split level.* Generally, a house that has floors halfway between other floors. One floor is often partially below ground level. Variations include *side-by-side split* and *multilevel split.*

• *Split-entry.* A modified split level. The entry is on grade or a few steps above, with the main level half a flight up and the lower level half a flight down.

• *Story-and-a-half.* Often called a *Cape Cod.* A low-profile house with a full flight of stairs connecting two levels. The roof line usually starts at the first story and peaks to allow headroom in about half of the second-story space.

• *Two-story.* Has two complete stories, both out of the ground, connected by a full flight of stairs. Entry is usually up a few steps from grade.

With these terms straight in your mind, you'll be ready for the next step—determining where and how to add on. *Opposite* are drawings of the five house types, with suggestions for several ways to add to each of them and how each addition works.

ADD-ON OPTIONS

RANCH

1. A basic rectangular ranch easily becomes an L. As shown in drawing 1a, you can expand an L-shaped ranch into a U or something more complex by building a second wing in front or back—or both.

2. On a small lot where there's no room for outward expansion, consider building a full second story for maximum additional space.

3. Put an addition atop your garage for a private aerie. You may have to add new interior stairs.

SPLIT LEVEL

4. One common way to expand a split level is to add at mid-level—if your lot is large enough. This kind of addition often extends out from one side of the original house.

5. A likely alternative is a one- or two-story addition at the back. This is especially good for a family room, since it gives access to the backyard.

SPLIT-ENTRY

6. Adding a single story to the entry level of a split-entry house gets you more living space and a new look outside.

7. Add a garage and a second floor to a split-entry for more space without altering existing floor levels. Again, the exterior view is drastically changed.

8. Add a one- or two-level addition to the back. This affects the exterior view the least and provides privacy as well as space.

STORY-AND-A-HALF

9. Add a one- or two-story structure at the rear of a story-and-a-half. Or, as shown in 9a, add space with a smaller ground-level addition at the rear, side, or front.

10. A shed dormer adds the most possible space. For an alcove in an existing room, try a conventional peaked dormer (not shown).

11. A second-floor addition over a garage is economical and especially works well for a bedroom or den.

TWO-STORY

12. An over-garage addition works well to bring more space to a two-story home.

13. Build on in front or back of a two-story, adding one or two extra stories as space needs dictate. For even more space and a symmetrical look, consider additions at either end of the original structure, or an addition that reaches the length of the house, as shown in 13a.

14. Add on at the side, wrapping around to front or back for extra space.

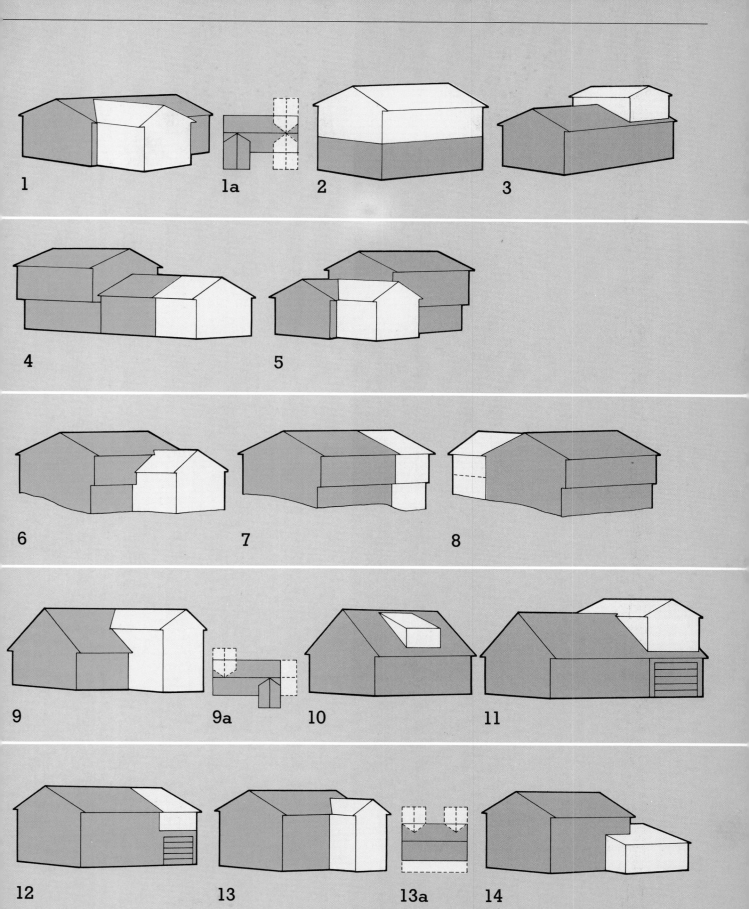

1

1a

2

3

4

5

6

7

8

9

9a

10

11

12

13

13a

14

ADDING OUT

As the preceding pages show, adding out to the front, back, or sides of a house is one of the most practical ways to add on. Once you decide to add out, you'll need to consider other things: making sure that your gained space doesn't bring awkward new proportions with it, tying the new roof to the old, laying new foundations, steering clear of lot lines, and extending or adding heating runs.

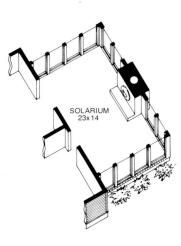

SOLARIUM
23x14

A dding out can make changes to your house that will turn it into a stranger—with luck and planning, a beautiful stranger. Before you start, however, be sure you're not creating a monster in place of your old, if too small, friend.

Your addition's exterior materials and style need not match, but should complement, those of the existing structure. For example, the exterior of this 14x23-foot solarium *above* has a contemporary look that contrasts nicely with the traditional two-story main house. Because this addition is small in relation to the house, its impact is relatively subtle.

For a larger or taller addition, decisions get more complex. How to deal with the roof is a major one. You can maintain the existing style and pitch. Or you can break away from the old roof line by building a passage from the old to the new section (especially useful for additions out of the mainstream of activity—bedroom suites, for example).

Belowground, consider what the addition's foundation would do to your home's surroundings. Here, for instance, it threatened tree roots. The solution was to slightly cantilever the new room. Before you set your heart on a particular location, check with a contractor about drainage, underground utility lines, and other matters that could affect your final decision.

Heating and cooling systems, although less visible than roofs, are also important. Many original systems are large enough to take on a new room or two, but check with a professional before you commit yourself. Be aware that although extending runs can be a simple job, extra bends and twists will reduce efficiency. Here existing ducts were easily extended, and this solarium absorbs enough winter sun to almost heat itself. *Opposite,* sun streams in through the skylight, as well as the windows. Leafy deciduous trees and a generous roof overhang help keep it cool in summer.

FITTING IN

ADDING UP

If your lot is too small, irregularly shaped, or steeply sloped to accommodate a left, right, front, or back addition, adding up may be for you. In fact, constructing a new roof and walls atop a house or garage is often less expensive and less time-consuming than building a similar structure at ground level. You don't need a new foundation—you can often rely on first-floor ceiling joists for support—and extending mechanical services upward is often easier than extending them horizontally.

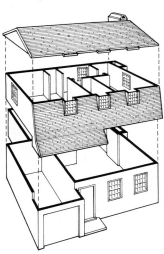

The Dutch Colonial house *at right* illustrates the ultimate in adding up. Once a stuccoed ranch, it reached new heights not by means of a simple dormer or an extra bedroom over the garage—both very good upward moves—but with an entire new level. The owner gained two bedrooms and a bath, for a total of 500 new square feet. The photos *above* show how the transformation occurred.

First the original roof and attic were removed. Then new framing was constructed to create a mansard roof that gives the home its new character.

Before you decide to tear the roof off your house, discuss with a contractor whether existing ceiling joists are strong enough to support the weight of another level. If not, you may need to replace or strengthen them.

In all but north-facing topside additions, incorporate as many windows as possible. This not only will make the new space pleasanter inside but also will help minimize the visual impact of an addition that might otherwise look top-heavy. Do be careful about spacing the new windows; they'll look best centered between or positioned directly over first-floor openings.

Plan access to second-story additions carefully. In the remodeling shown here, a stairway in the living room leads upstairs without taking up excessive floor space. You may be able to use existing attic stairs, or cut a doorway through an existing wall, but chances are you'll simply have to add a new set of stairs. Circular stairs require a little less space than conventional stairs but may be a hazard for small children or the elderly.

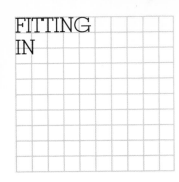

ADDING ON
FROM THE
INSIDE OUT

Most additions not only change the way you live inside your home, they also give you a chance to take—and create—a new look outdoors. Once you've begun to think about your home's floor plan, it's natural to go on to your whole lot, looking for better ways to use and organize space, whether for children's play, family entertaining, or service and storage. On this and the next three pages, we'll show you how an addition can do as much for your outdoor living space as it does indoors.

The luxurious master bedroom wing pictured *at left* is only part of the add-on project the owners devised for their house. A sheltered tile patio, complete with swimming pool and privacy screen, is an integral part of the new quarters. Broad steps lead directly to the patio, and in cool or wet weather, the owners can still enjoy a great view across the pool, thanks to floor-to-ceiling windows.

View, access, and privacy are among the most important aspects to consider when you want your addition to work as well outside as inside. If you have the space, a deck, active game area, or swimming pool may be an ideal finishing touch. In fact, a new wing may act as a giant privacy screen, making your outdoor living area even more enjoyable.

The size and shape of your lot are important factors in determining how your outdoor space will tie in with your new interior space. If you have an unusual lot, such as the wedge at the head of a cul-de-sac, or a rectangle with a service alley at the back, your privacy and space-juggling needs will require extra creativity.

On a more conventional mid-block lot with other properties on three sides and a street in front, one option is to design a game court or patio to be reached directly from a rear addition. Shrubbery or fencing on one or more sides will create a greater sense of seclusion.

A corner lot means you have one less neighbor, but an extra street. If you're adding on at right angles to the house, you can create a secluded outdoor area in the angle between the house and the addition. *(continued)*

FITTING IN

ADDING ON FROM THE INSIDE OUT
(continued)

When you build an addition, you may discover that you've changed the landscaping orientation of your entire lot. A new extension can eliminate a row of shrubbery, block a view, or draw the eye to a previously unnoticed flower bed. A raised roof or dormer may give a house so much height that the surrounding greenery looks disproportionately small, or give a once-small house the dignity it's always needed to stand up to the tall trees around it.

The changes resulting from your adding-on project may be major enough to lead you to consult a landscape professional. But whether you do that or decide to handle the consequences yourself, here are some things to think about before you start any work.

• Make a rough sketch of preaddition landscaping so you can see how certain features line up in relation to your house. Some trees or shrubs may be expendable.

• Note how your landscaping works from inside the house. Do doors already lead directly to a patio? Do windows provide an attractive view of gardens or trees? If so, you may want to avoid blocking them, or else replace them with equally desirable plantings.

• Consider how your house looks to the outside world. Do you need additional privacy screens? If you don't have fences, hedges, or other screening now, will you need to add them when the addition is complete, to shield the newly created living areas?

If you conclude that your landscaping is one of the best features of your house, you'll want to be especially careful about how you plan your addition. Ideally, any new structure will take full advantage of attractive outdoor features. The add-on kitchen/breakfast room *at left,* for example, is tailor-made for its nature-oriented owners. There's a view from almost every side of the interestingly angled structure. (A bird feeder tucked into a windowed nook in the facade is a special extra here.) Railroad-tie terracing relates the addition to the backyard landscape, and a new deck extends off the breakfast/sitting end of the new space. Steps (see plan) lead to the yard from the deck, making the new indoor space and the outdoor space surrounding it into one cohesive and delightfully livable unit.

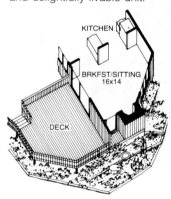

KITCHEN

BRKFST/SITTING
16x14

DECK

FITTING IN

FURNISHING AN ADDITION

Empty spaces, however exciting they may be, don't make a house, or an addition, a home. This happens once the construction's over and you and your furniture move into the great new space you've created. But before you fill up those spaces, consider this: Is the addition visible from the rest of the house, or is it a more isolated unit? Do you want to continue the decorating themes of the rest of your house, or do you want a change of pace? Does new space immediately make you think of new furniture, or do you want to move old furnishings in and redo another room? Once you decide, you'll be on the way to a successful decorating adventure.

The exterior of your addition is going to be seen in conjunction with the rest of your house, so it's important that the two blend well together. The same may or may not be true of the interior.

If your addition opens up from another room and is in constant view from elsewhere in the house, you'll probably want to tie it in to your existing decorating scheme. For example, the gracious add-on dining room shown *opposite* opens onto the equally warm and elegant living room pictured *above*. By using related styles of furniture in each room, the owners tied the new area to the living room without giving up the variety and detail that make the whole so appealing.

The view from the living room into the addition shows how traditional furnishings, highlighted by a contemporary touch or two, effectively integrate old and new. For example, an ultra-modern commercial light fixture contrasts with the Shaker-style cherry dining table. The glossy new oak floor looks like a continuation of the living room floor and adds to the unified effect.

A new look for new space
If your addition will be visually separate from other rooms—or if you're just in the mood for something different—you have a great opportunity to experiment. Maybe a new family room is exactly the place to try modular seating and bold wall

graphics, even if the rest of your house is cozily traditional. Or a new master bedroom wing may be just right for the small country prints that are too dainty for the more actively lived-in rooms of your house.

Mix and match
Now is a good time to look at furniture in other parts of your house—including the attic. You may be able to find a home for unused or underused pieces. Or, try moving furniture from other rooms into the addition and concentrating your purchasing efforts elsewhere. For example, if you've built a family room especially for the kids, you could transfer the much-used living room sofa there and treat the grownups to new living room seating.

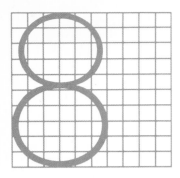

EXTERIOR SURFACE MATERIALS

Whether you're adding a dormer or building an entire wing, the exterior surface materials you choose may very well make the difference between a merely serviceable addition and one that also adds to your home's good looks. As we explained in the previous chapter, an addition can either match your home's present appearance or complement it with different materials. Here you'll find information about a wide array of siding and roofing materials, as well as paints and stains to protect and color them.

MANUFACTURED SIDING

Survey the homes pictured *opposite*. Can you see how they look different from houses sided with wood or other natural materials? Probably not. Nearly all manmade materials today are very convincing imitations of the real thing.

What makes manufactured sidings different is that they are easier to maintain and/or less expensive than their natural counterparts. The first manufactured siding material, asbestos-cement shingles, was intended to look like wood, brick, or stone—but fooled almost no one. Manufactured sidings have come a long way since then. Today you can choose among hardboard, metal, vinyl, and other products, many with lengthy guarantees. Here's how these products compare.

Hardboard
Hardboard, a wood-fiber product, is one of the least expensive sidings. It's easy to install and can look like real wood. Textures range from rough to smooth; some selections contain a prefinished wood grain resembling fir or cedar.

Hardboard siding comes in panels for vertical installation and strips for horizontal lapping. Preprimed hardboard requires paint; vinyl-clad doesn't. Typically, lap siding units measure 1 foot by 16 feet and are $7/16$ inch thick. Panels are 4 feet wide by 8, 9, or 10 feet long.

Metal
Aluminum and steel siding come in both panel and lap forms. Each metal is fireproof and requires little maintenance. Steel siding is more resistant to denting and scratching; it also costs more. If the enamel or vinyl coating on metal siding is scratched, you should touch up or repaint; otherwise corrosion will set in.

Unit sizes vary, but strips typically measure 4 to 8 inches wide and 12 to 13 feet long. Vertical units come in the same widths and range from 8 to 12 feet high.

Metal strips don't retain moisture and are not affected by termites. Metal siding conducts electricity and therefore must be grounded to protect against lightning.

Vinyl
Extruded into a variety of colors, shapes, sizes, and textures, vinyl siding is increasingly popular. It is a little easier to work with than metal and resists heat and cold better. However, temperature extremes cause expansion and contraction, which must be allowed for when vinyl is installed. Because color permeates the siding all the way through, scratches are hardly noticeable; in fact, vinyl cannot be repainted.

Sand-spray
Most manufactured sidings simulate the appearance of natural wood, but sand-spray has its own distinctive appearance. A plywood that has been coated with epoxy-held sand, it more closely resembles masonry. Sand-spray siding is widely used in the Southwest, and is sometimes called Texture-111. *(continued)*

MANUFACTURED SIDING
(continued)

YOUR MANUFACTURED SIDING OPTIONS

TYPES	EFFECTS

HARDBOARD

Hardboard lap or panel siding comes in a variety of prefinished colors, textures, and sizes. Unfinished hardboard requires prime and finish coats; some is preprimed and needs only a finish coat. Vinyl-clad is ready to use.

Hardboard siding looks like everything but hardboard. Aside from rough, smooth, and knotty wood imitations, hardboard also can duplicate stucco and exposed aggregate finishes.

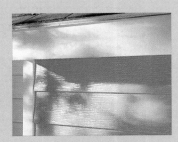

METAL

Metal offers an array of textures and finishes, including baked-on enamel, vinyl, and other laminated treatments. Aluminum and steel sidings consist of vertically or horizontally installed strips or panels that lock together.

Like hardboard, metal siding also imitates wood in appearance. Aluminum comes in a wide range of lap or vertical, even shingle and shake styles; steel choices are more limited. Insulated steel and aluminum sidings are available.

VINYL

Your choice of textures and colors is narrower than with other sidings.

Maintenance on vinyl siding is practically nil; only an occasional hosing off is necessary to retain a fresh new look.

SAND-SPRAY

Sand-spray combines aggregate and 4x8-foot sheets of plywood. Three aggregate sizes are used; the smallest is rough sand. Panels can be purchased in a variety of earth-tone colors.

Light-colored sand-spray panels reflect the intense summer sunlight typically found in semiarid regions such as the Southwest.

DURABILITY	USES	INSTALLATION	COST
When refinished every five years, grade "A" preprimed hardboard siding should last 15 to 25 years. Grade "B" deteriorates sooner, often because of moisture penetration. Vinyl-clad hardboard carries guarantees up to 30 years.	Good low- to moderate-budget exterior wall covering for homes and additions.	Easiest to install, lap or panel siding can be applied to sheathed or unsheathed exterior walls where studs are on 16-inch centers. Metal corners available for lap siding; other trim work can be done using strips of wood or hardboard.	Unfinished and preprimed is inexpensive to moderate, depending upon the grade. Vinyl-clad is the most costly of hardboard sidings.
Manufacturers' warranties start at 25 years. In some cases, such as with some specially laminated steel sidings, the warranty is for the lifetime of the house.	Excellent for both re-siding jobs and new construction. Keep in mind that aluminum siding can be dented by hail.	Consists of vertically and horizontally installed units that interlock, as well as numerous accessories, including soffit and fascia treatments. Installation is best left to a professional siding installer.	Aluminum ranks as a medium-price siding; top-quality steel siding is the most expensive manufactured siding on the market.
Because of contraction and expansion, vinyl siding can look wavy on the wall; it also has been known to fade. Overall, however, it holds up well, never needs repainting, and often comes with a 40-year warranty.	Re-siding and new construction.	As with metal sidings, when you purchase solid vinyl siding, you purchase a somewhat sophisticated siding system that can be tricky to assemble. Professional installation is recommended.	Moderate to expensive.
Manufacturers claim that sand-spray can last for the life of the house with proper installation.	New construction only.	Professionally installed sand-spray panels go up much as plywood panels do. It is important for joints between panels to be thoroughly caulked before battens are applied.	Moderate.

NATURAL WOOD SIDING

Wood shingles and lapped siding have been around since colonial times. More recently, they've been joined by plywood panels. Now all three are part of the American building tradition—and nothing can quite match the look of wood in certain settings. With proper installation and maintenance, wood is highly durable, too. Here and on the following two pages, we'll tell you about a wide range of wood sidings.

The photographs *opposite* show wood siding at its varied best. From the contemporary look of stained wood panels and the mellow warmth of weathered shingles and barnboard to the neatly finished order of well-maintained clapboards, wood is at home on nearly any house.

As an exterior cover over new construction, wood can either match an existing treatment or provide an appealing contrast with other coverings such as brick, stone, and stucco. Another plus about wood is its workability. Unlike manufactured siding systems, which often require professional installation, wood siding and trim can be installed by an experienced do-it-yourselfer.

Lap siding
Wood lap siding comes in an assortment of species, including redwood, cedar, cypress, fir, and pine. All-heart (cut from the center of logs) and clear (knot-free) grades of redwood, cedar, and cypress resist termites and decay.

Textures are limited, ranging from wood-grain smooth to feathery rough-sawn. Lapping styles, however, offer a broad selection: The most familiar is the traditional *clapboard*.

Clapboard consists of overlapping boards of random length and equal thickness that are applied horizontally. Variations on this overlapping style include *beveled* wood siding, *rabbeted* or *shiplapped* siding, and *tongue-and-groove (car) siding*. Some of these styles can be applied vertically or even diagonally. Strictly vertical styles include *board and batten* (boards with narrow strips covering the joints between them), *board on board*

(equal-width boards lapped about 1 inch), and *reverse board and batten* (narrow batten strips go up first, then the boards are staggered overtop). The house shown *opposite, lower left* is clad with board and batten siding.

To finish wood lap siding, choose a durable acrylic latex paint, stain, or other high-quality sealer. If you use redwood, cedar, or cypress, you can let the wood weather naturally or hasten the weathering process and achieve consistent coloration by applying bleaching oil.

Plywood siding
Plywood siding ranks as a favorite among builders. The panels, which measure 4 feet wide and 8, 9, or 10 feet long, install quickly and easily. Because each panel covers at least 32 square feet of exterior wall surface, a small building crew can side an entire house in a single day.

Like wood lap siding, plywood panels are available in redwood, fir, cedar, and pine. Textures range from smooth to rough, with a multitude of machined surface patterns, including splintery rough-sawn, striated, corrugated, V-grooved, board and batten, and reverse board and batten.

To preserve and highlight the wood's grain and texture, select a transparent or semitransparent stain. For solid color, use a heavy-bodied opaque stain or coat the panels with an acrylic or alkyd paint.

MDO plywood
With a smooth, resin-coated, wood-fiber surface bonded to plywood, MDO (medium density overlay) plywood combines the good painting surface of hardboard siding with the strength of plywood. Couple

this with MDO's varied texture treatments, which resemble those of plywood and hardboard, and you have a siding that's hard to beat.

Like other plywood sidings, MDO comes in standard 4x8-foot sheets; you also can buy 9- and 10-foot lengths. Its tough surface, available either finished or unfinished, is especially resistant to woodpeckers and other pests.

Shingles and shakes
Of all the sidings available, none offers a warmer, friendlier look than wood shingles or shakes. And cedar—the wood that shingles and shakes are made from—is also a good insulator.

Shingles are sawed; shakes are hand-split. Consequently, shakes are thicker and striated or grooved on at least one side. Both shingles and shakes have a beveled shape and typically range in length from 18 to 24 inches.

When applying shingles or shakes to sidewalls, choose a single- or double-course installation. With double-coursing, you nail up two layers, one on top of the other; this improves insulation and weather-tightness, and also creates deep, dramatic course lines.

Let cedar shingles and shakes weather naturally, or paint or stain them. It's a good idea to treat them with a mildewcide to prevent moss buildup. *(continued)*

NATURAL WOOD SIDING
(continued)

YOUR WOOD SIDING OPTIONS

TYPES	EFFECTS

WOOD LAP
Random-length wood sidings are available in cedar, redwood, cypress, fir, and pine. Styles include clapboard, beveled, shiplapped, tongue-and-groove (car) siding, and board and batten.

Left to weather naturally or with bleaching oil, wood lap siding allows any house or addition to blend into natural surroundings. Paint or stain the surfaces, and you can play up the smooth or coarse textures and grains found in natural wood itself.

PLYWOOD
Panels come unfinished in many textures and patterns, including rough and smooth, striated, corrugated, reverse board and batten, and grooved. Buy 4x8-, 4x9-, or 4x10-foot panels in thicknesses from 5/16 to 3/4 inch.

Rustic plywood panels offer the same desirable natural-wood look as wood lap siding. And equally important, because a plywood siding application results in fewer joints, the chance of cold air infiltrating behind the siding is minimized.

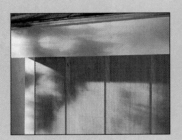

MDO PLYWOOD
Panels are available in smooth and rough embossed textures, with or without grooving, unfinished or pre-primed. Length and width are the same sizes as ordinary plywood; thicknesses vary from 11/32 to 5/8 inch.

The hard coating of this siding permits it to resist severe weather better than most sidings. MDO doesn't chip or dent, and its ability to hold paint better than ordinary plywood makes it highly desirable.

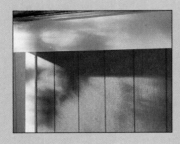

SHINGLES AND SHAKES
Cedar shingles have a smooth surface; shakes are textured. Shingles typically are unfinished when purchased, though some come with factory-applied colors. Lengths run 16, 18, and 24 inches; widths and thicknesses vary.

Reminiscent of early American saltbox- and Cape Cod-style homes, shingles and shakes offer a homey look that stands up well against even the most severe weather. Cedar shingles and shakes offer thermal insulation and resist moisture penetration and attacks by termites. When applied to an addition, they can weather naturally, or be bleached, painted, or stained.

DURABILITY	USES	INSTALLATION	COST
Some types (pine and fir) require occasional refinishing; redwood, cedar, and cypress can weather naturally yet resist rot and termites. With proper installation and maintenance, all wood lap siding can last the life of the house.	New sidewall construction of homes, additions, and garages.	Fastens easily to sidewalls; trims out with wood. Sidewalls should have a vapor barrier; siding that is not naturally rot-resistant should be sealed with a clear water repellent, bleaching oil, pigmented stain, or latex or oil paint.	Inexpensive to expensive, depending on the species of wood. Pine is the least expensive; redwood, the most.
Occasional refinishing necessary with all plywood sidings, except those that can weather naturally. With proper care, plywood siding can last the life of the house, though warranties average around 15 years.	New sidewall construction of homes, additions, and garages.	Depending on thickness, apply panels over sheathing or studs. To avoid installing sheathing, use ½-, ⅝-, or ¾-inch panels (not 5/16- or ⅜-inch thicknesses). Provide a vapor barrier and seal panels. Caulk joints.	Inexpensive to moderate.
Because of its special resin-treated surface, MDO can retain a finish longer than wood and hardboard sidings, and therefore requires less maintenance. With proper care, it will last the life of the house.	Good for new sidewall construction, especially in regions that experience extremes in temperature.	Installs like plywood.	Expensive.
In regions of high heat and humidity, cedar shingles and shakes should be treated with a mildewcide. With proper installation, they should last the life of the house.	Sidewalls and roofs.	Can be homeowner-installed. Apply shingles and shakes in either single or double courses on tar-paper-covered sheathing. Limit exposure to between 7½ and 8 inches and include a vapor barrier.	Moderate to expensive, depending on the type of application and grade of shingles and shakes used.

MASONRY

No exterior surfacing material comes close to matching the permanence of brick, slump stone, natural stone, or stucco—and only a few can match their beauty. As you'll see here and on pages 120 and 121, masonry materials offer not only durability and solidity but a wide variety of colors, textures, and bonding patterns. Add to this their fire resistance and low maintenance, and you have a first-class covering for an addition.

Selecting the masonry material and look you want for your addition starts with paging through building magazines and studying neighborhoods you think are attractive. Then visit local brickyards, stone suppliers, and home centers to find out what is available in your area. More than with other types of exterior surfacing, the availability of specific masonry materials varies by region, although suppliers may be able to special-order unstocked items for you.

The look each type of masonry exterior adds to a home is highly varied, too. For example, the brick and stone veneers *opposite, top* lend a warm, traditional touch to the two homes shown, although the brick house is certainly contemporary in other aspects of its design. In contrast, the squared-off house *opposite, bottom* is distinctly modern, and its concrete exterior is in keeping with that geometric approach.

Years ago homes were built of solid masonry. Nowadays, most have only an exterior veneer applied over sheathing and conventional stud construction. However, many building codes require heavier footings to bear the extra weight—a factor that must be taken into account when you're comparing costs to other siding materials.

Consider also that you'll probably want to hire a professional mason to complete this portion of the construction. Most masonry work, except laying brick, calls for tools, techniques, and brawn that are beyond most do-it-yourselfers.

Slump stone

Made to look like natural stone, slump stone is a light-weight brick or block composed of cement (or other adhesive material) and straw, or fiber glass. Once removed from its mold, a slump stone unit assumes a softly rectangular shape which results in a contoured, somewhat irregular block face.

Available in a range of colors, textures, and sizes, slump stone is found most frequently in the southwestern United States. It protects homeowners from the hot, dry climate the same way adobe bricks do.

Related to manufactured slump stones are the thin, lightweight brick and stone veneers that are also made from cement. Typically, these products have one outward-facing side that's real stone or brick.

Buy both slump stone and thin lightweight veneers by the square foot. When you buy the thin veneers, you also have to buy corner pieces.

Natural stone

Made from tightly bonded minerals, natural building stone offers a variety of textures, colors, and shapes. Some stone types come as angular chunks; others are rough-sawn into square and rectangular blocks; still others are flat with a patterned, machined surface.

Natural stone falls into one of three general classifications. *Igneous* rock, originating as molten rock, hardens into well-known types such as granite and traprock. *Sedimentary* stone, formed by the layering of seashells, sand, and other sediments, is found in massive sprawling deposits of limestone and sandstone. *Metamorphic* stone is igneous or sedimentary stone that has been changed under heat and pressure. Marble, slate, gneiss, and quartzite are metamorphic stones.

Brick

Manufactured from clays and shales and fired in giant kilns, brick comes in a variety of earth tones. Textures are also diverse, ranging from smooth to stippled, sanded, even deliberately roughened for a rustic, always-been-there look.

Brick dimensions vary by type. The most common type is modular brick, which is 8 inches long and 4 inches high. (These measurements include a ½-inch mortar joint on the bottom and one side.)

Stucco

Not quite as enduring as natural stone or brick, stucco is nonetheless a sound masonry alternative. It outlasts many other exterior materials and requires little maintenance.

Stucco is made from masonry cement and sand spread on exterior walls in two or three ⅛-inch coats. You can apply it in any of several patterns, including smooth, swirled, wavy, stippled, and travertine.

If you don't like the light gray of natural stucco, add pigment to the ingredients. Or simply paint or stain your stucco. For a dazzling white stucco, mix white portland cement, lime, and white silica sand. *(continued)*

YOUR MASONRY OPTIONS

TYPES	EFFECTS

SLUMP STONE
Fashioned into blocks from cement and straw, or fiber glass, this material comes in several sizes and surface textures. Related products are thin lightweight brick and stone veneers.

Widely used in hot, dry climates, slump stone keeps a home's interior cool and looks like adobe brick. Pigments can be introduced into the cement to produce a color that blends with its surroundings.

NATURAL STONE
Natural stone is sold in square feet as *rubble* stone (broken or rounded pieces) or *ashlar* (square or rectangular blocks, *at left)*. Types include granite, traprock, limestone, sandstone, schist, gneiss, marble, slate, quartzite.

Natural stone walls offer beauty and permanence. Used on both contemporary and traditional homes, stone is an excellent windbreak and offers perhaps the widest range of color possibilities, including variegated combinations of natural hues.

BRICK
Facing brick, the common choice for veneer work, comes in a wide assortment of colors and finishes. Dimensions also vary, depending on the specific brick types.

The geometric bonding patterns, textures, and color combinations available in brick make it one of the most adaptable of all cladding materials. It looks good with everything—lap and panel sidings, stucco, and stone. Brick's many coarse lines break up the heavy, solid-wall look and offer in its place lightness, depth, and interesting designs.

STUCCO
A mortarlike material made from cement and sand, stucco can be pigmented and textured in any one of several styles.

Stucco's many texture possibilities are its most notable aesthetic feature. A smooth white finish appears iridescent and helps deflect summer sunlight and heat. A swirl texture, on the other hand, creates deep, rich shadows. Wood trim, such as stained rough-sawn cedar, is especially effective for framing and accenting stucco walls.

DURABILITY	USES	INSTALLATION	COST
Slump stone requires no maintenance and lasts the life of the house.	Good exterior cladding in new construction. Also works well for other outdoor structures—planters, tree wells, and barbecues—and decorative interior treatments, including fireplaces.	Professionally installed, slump stone is laid in mortar. Joints are often not smoothed. A sound support system, including a footing, is necessary for a lasting, structurally strong wall.	Moderate compared to other masonry coverings, but availability is limited.
An enduring covering that requires no maintenance and lasts the life of the structure.	Used as part or all of an exterior wall treatment in new construction. Excellent for landscaping structures and interior accent work, including fireplaces.	Natural stone veneer should be professionally applied by a stone mason. Here, too, a solid footing must be provided.	Expensive.
An enduring material that requires no maintenance and lasts the life of the house.	Used for exterior walls and interior accent work, including fireplaces. Bricks also are used in garden walls, patios, and other decorative outside structures.	Either a skilled homeowner with the right tools and instructions or a professional bricklayer can lay brick veneer. Mortared bricks, like stone, must have a firm footing.	Moderate to expensive (depending on whether a professional bricklayer does the work).
When correctly applied, stucco should last the life of the house. A watered-down stucco or poor bonding surface could result in flaking. You can paint or stain stucco to preserve a fresh look on the exterior.	Stucco is primarily a decorative wall covering for exterior walls. Also use it for interior walls and accent work.	With proper instructions, a skilled homeowner can handle the work, but the job is best left to a professional. Stucco is applied to either concrete block or plywood sheathing covered with wire lath.	Least expensive per square foot of all masonry coverings.

PAINTS AND STAINS

If you choose masonry, redwood, cedar, or many manufactured siding materials, you can just put them up and forget about them. Other sidings must be protected from moisture and sunlight. For these, the coating you choose can be almost as important as the material itself. Otherwise, you could be faced with a costly re-siding job in just a few years. If the siding on your addition matches the original house, you'll probably want to use the same brand name, type of coating, and color. If you're interested in an all-new look, here are your options.

The more time, effort, and money you pour into a sealing, staining, or painting project, the more you're going to get out of it. To begin with, buy the kind of finish that performs best with your type of siding and climate (see the chart on pages 124 and 125). The few dollars more you spend on quality will mean you don't have to recoat your walls quite as soon as you otherwise would.

When figuring material needs, calculate the number of square feet of wall surface—minus openings—that you'll need to cover. With lap siding, add 10 percent; for shingles, 20 percent; highly porous masonry and stucco can soak up as much as 50 percent more. If you'll be using a brush or roller, add yet another 10 percent to allow for waste; if you'll be spraying, add 25 percent. Now divide your final result by 400—the number of square feet normally covered by a gallon of stain or paint. This gives you the number of gallons you must buy.

Good wall preparation is another key to long-lasting protection. Paint manufacturers recommend applying sealers, stains, and paints over clean, dry surfaces. Dirt or moisture behind the finish not only will mar the appearance but also could cause bubbling and cracking later on.

To ensure excellent drying conditions, avoid applying a finish during unfavorable weather. Ideally, temperatures should be moderate (around 50 to 70 degrees) without any threat of rain in the forecast.

During application, remember to coat all edges and end grains. If you're painting, apply primer prior to applying finish coats. For more specific instructions, see the manufacturer's label on the can.

Here's a rundown of what you'll find when you visit your favorite paint supplier.

Paint

For playing down blemishes or creating an interesting color scheme, like the one *opposite, below,* there is no substitute for exterior house paint. Applied in two coats over a companion primer made by the same manufacturer, paint provides protection that can make wood and other sidings last almost indefinitely.

The most common house paints today are *alkyd-based* and *water-thinned latex* paints. Alkyd is a "chalking" paint that sheds dirt by gradually eroding with each rain. (Note that true "oil-base" house paints are rarely sold anymore, though you may hear paint store personnel referring to alkyds as oil paints.) Water-thinned latex is a fast-drying coating that expands and contracts and permits the release of moisture from the siding to the outside. This means that you can apply latex over slightly damp surfaces.

Though not for siding, you also can buy glossy *trim enamel* paint for exterior surfaces that undergo considerable wear such as around windows and doors. Trim paint also is available in both alkyd and latex varieties.

Semitransparent stain

Ideal for enhancing wood grains and textures, oil-base, semitransparent stain preserves wood as well as paint does. Whether it's used on siding, as shown *opposite, upper left,* shakes, or shingles, semitransparent stain applies quickly and easily. In addition, it resists fading and bleeding. Typically, two coats are required for a rich tinting, though you can get by with just one.

The main drawback of semitransparent stain is that it will not neutralize color variations in the wood or hide repairs such as filled knotholes.

Heavy-bodied stain

Known also as *opaque* stain, heavy-bodied stain—which can have either an oil or latex base—offers the advantages of both paint and stain. Like paint, it provides a solid color, but it also permits wood's texture to show through, as stain does. Heavy-bodied stain applies easily and does a terrific job of covering knots and coloration differences often found in wood.

Clear finishes

Because many of the wood grains and textures are highly appealing, you may choose to maintain their natural look with a nonfilming, clear wood *preservative* and/or *sealer.* Made from linseed oil, pentachlorophenol, or phenylmercury oleate, products in this category work to discourage fungus, ward off insects, and provide waterproofing. *Urethane* and *spar* varnishes offer moisture protection and a glossy finish. Another option, *bleaching oil,* accelerates an even weathered look on wood siding—achieving it in just a few months. Bleaching oil was used to achieve the striking, silvery appearance of the oceanfront house shown *opposite, upper right.* The one problem with clear sealers is that they break down sooner than stain and paint, and therefore require refinishing sooner.

(continued)

PAINTS
AND STAINS
(continued)

YOUR PAINT AND STAIN OPTIONS

TYPES   **EFFECTS**

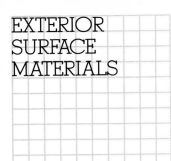

PAINT
The two main types are latex, which is thinned with water, and alkyd, which requires a solvent for cleanup.

Paint provides the widest choice of colors of any exterior surface coating and works especially well on smooth surfaces. It also protects sidings such as wood and hardboard from moisture damage and rot. Applied over metal sidings and a suitable primer, paint prevents rust and corrosion.

SEMITRANSPARENT STAIN
Oil-base, semitransparent stain penetrates the surface, comes in a great variety of tints, and can be made richer looking by double-coating.

Semitransparent stain provides a thin, tinted window that permits you to see the true natural surface, allows the wood to breathe, and does not trap moisture. Some stains include a preservative for woods susceptible to rot or termites.

HEAVY-BODIED STAIN
Heavy-bodied or opaque stain comes with either a latex or oil base and is available in numerous colors.

Unlike penetrating stain, heavy-bodied stain masks natural wood grain. But it allows texture to show through and adheres well to a variety of surfaces. This deeply pigmented type of stain does an excellent job of making knots, repairs, and other blemishes disappear. If you plan to use a heavy-bodied stain, you can purchase lesser grades of siding, since minor flaws are no longer a problem.

CLEAR SEALER
Bleaching and linseed oils, urethane and spar varnishes, pentachlorophenol, and phenylmercury oleate produce clear finishes.

No other paint products let you display the natural look of your wood the way clear sealer can. With clear sealer, every grain, knot, and texture treatment becomes visible for all to see and enjoy. Urethane and spar varnish hold wood's graying and weathering tendency in check; the other sealers permit it. Bleaching oil, in fact, actually speeds the process. Many sealers, which are made primarily to seal and protect wood, also work effectively as mildewcides.

DURABILITY	USES	INSTALLATION	COST
Repainting, on the average, is needed every five years. Alkyds are slightly more durable than latex.	Typically applied over smooth exterior sidings, including wood, hardboard, and metal; some latex paints also can be used on shingles and shakes.	Done by professional house painters or homeowners, paint can be applied with a sprayer, brush, or roller. Latex dries faster than alkyd. With both, proper priming is a must.	Moderate to expensive. Exterior house paint prices begin where those for interior paints end. (Previously unpainted materials can soak up a surprising amount of paint.)
Fair (though two coats will hold up as well as paint).	Excellent on rough wood sidings, trim, shingles, and shakes.	Easier than paint. Done by professional house painters or homeowners, penetrating stain can be applied with a sprayer, brush, or roller. No primer needed.	Moderate.
Good. Heavy-bodied latex stain retains its color longer, but heavy-bodied oil stain acts as a better preservative.	Protects and colors coarse or smooth wood panel and lap sidings, wood shingles, and shakes.	Done by professional house painters or homeowners, heavy-bodied stain can be applied with a sprayer, brush, or roller. No primer necessary.	Moderate.
Poor to fair (some sealers and varnishes only last a few years).	Sealers work well on coarse and smooth panel and lap wood sidings, wood shingles and shakes, and exterior trim. Use varnishes only on smooth wood sidings and trim.	Done by professional house painters or homeowners, clear sealers can be applied with a sprayer, brush, or roller.	Inexpensive (bleaching oil) to expensive (urethane and spar varnish).

ROOFING

The way you cap off your new addition will have a lot to do with its success. Whether you choose a roofing material identical to what's on your existing structure—which is what most homeowners do—or use a different material, the final result must harmonize with your overall color scheme and house design. For this reason, the choice of a roofing treatment should not be a spur-of-the-moment decision. There are, as you'll see here and on the following two pages, many things to consider.

The roof of any house is probably the architectural element most vulnerable to the weather. Sunlight is a roof's number one enemy. It causes asphalt shingles to buckle and break up over time. Assaults by rain wear the granules off asphalt shingles and make wooden shingles and shakes warp, split, and rot. Snow and ice bring frost that can work members of slate and tile roofs loose.

Of all the characteristics to look for in a roofing material, durability is the most important. Although buying quality may cost more at the beginning, you'll be dollars ahead by not having to pay for new materials and a second or third roofing job later on.

When you select a color for your roof, consider your location. If you live in a southern climate where there's plenty of sunshine, your best choice is a light-colored roof that reflects the sun's rays and maintains coolness within the structure. If you live in a more wintry or wooded region, select a dark roof that will absorb heat and/or blend in with rustic surroundings.

The size and pattern of the individual shingles, shakes, or tiles also should be compatible with the new and existing structures.

Keep in mind, too, that the way you top off a flat roof is quite different from how you deal with a sloped roof. If the *pitch* or incline of the roof falls below 4 inches of rise per foot, you're better off going with roll asphalt roofing for maximum waterproofing. On a flat roof, achieve protection by having a professional roofer lay the roof with roofing felt and then coat the felt with hot-mopped tar and gravel. On a sloped roof, your options include asphalt and asphalt/fiber-glass shingles, wood shingles and shakes, clay tile and slate, and metal roofing.

Whatever your choice, make sure the roofing material offers adequate resistance to fire. Asphalt/fiber-glass shingles, for instance, have an exceedingly high fire-resistant rating; wood shingles and shakes—unless they have been specially treated—offer no fire resistance at all.

Consider the weight of your roofing material. In the case of clay tile or slate, you sometimes need a stronger roofing support system to hold the extra load.

Roofing material is sold by the square, or the amount of roofing it takes to cover 100 square feet of area. In arriving at a final cost figure, don't forget to figure in the roofing felt underlayment necessary for all roofing.

Asphalt

The most popular roofing material, asphalt covers the roofs of 80 percent of America's homes, including the one pictured *opposite, upper left.* Made from asphalt-saturated felt and coated with mineral granules, this product comes in countless colors and several patterns, and is available in three basic forms: 12x36-inch asphalt shingles; similarly sized asphalt/fiber-glass shingles; and 3x6-foot rolls of asphalt roofing.

Wood shingles and shakes

Like shingle and shake siding (see pages 114-117), these coverings are machine-cut or hand-split from cedar to 16- to 24-inch lengths and random widths. They come either finished or unfinished; can be clear-sealed (like those shown *opposite, upper right),* stained, or painted; and can be treated with mildewcides and fire retardants for added protection.

Clay tile and slate

Roofing tiles are made of kiln-fired clay. Some are molded into half-cylinders; others resemble shingles and slates. Roofing slates are flat, quarried, and machine-cut rectangles or squares. Purchase slate in gray, green, and red; clay tile in several earth-tone colors. Both tile and slate are very durable, fire-resistant, and attractive, but they are also brittle, heavy, difficult to repair, and costly.

Metal roofing

Metal roofing is typically aluminum. It comes in corrugated or ribbed sheets and in striated shingles that closely resemble wood shingles or shakes. The sheets often come unfinished; the shingles are almost always factory-painted. Sheet metal can be utilitarian and economical, or as elegant as the squared dome shown *opposite, below,* but it generally looks like metal, no matter what the setting. *(continued)*

ROOFING
(continued)

YOUR ROOFING OPTIONS

TYPES	**EFFECTS**

ASPHALT

Traditional asphalt shingles are made of roofing felt saturated with asphalt and coated with mineral granules; newer types may have a fiber-glass base. Asphalt roofing also comes in rolls.

Asphalt shingles come in a wide variety of colors and styles. Extra-thick ones cast the deep shadows characteristic of wood shakes and shingles.

WOOD SHINGLES AND SHAKES

Cedar shingles are smooth; hand-split shakes have a striated surface. Though shingles typically are unfinished when purchased, some styles come factory-colored.

Few roofings can compete with cedar shingles and shakes for charm. The deep course lines created by the ½- to ¾-inch thickness of the exposed ends provide plenty of dimension and beauty. Left to weather to a gray color or treated with a colored stain or paint, cedar roofing readily blends into its surroundings.

CLAY TILES AND SLATES

Clay tiles are kiln-fired ceramic half-cylinders or shingles; roofing slates are quarried and cut into flat rectangles or squares.

Clay tile and slate are very attractive. The soft colors and varied texture of these roofing materials add to the interest of almost any structure without being obtrusive.

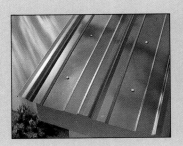

METAL

Metal roofings include *stainless steel* and *copper,* but *aluminum* is by far the most common. Shingles and corrugated, ribbed, or flat strips up to 30 feet long are available.

Metal roofs can be left natural or painted a light color to reflect sunlight and keep structures cool. Dark paint has the opposite effect. Sheet-metal roofing is often thought of as strictly functional, but more decorative metal roofs that imitate other materials in appearance are increasingly available.

DURABILITY	USES	INSTALLATION	COST
15-30 years (asphalt/fiber-glass shingles last the longest). Interlocking tabs or self-adhering strips that bond when heated by the sun help resist even hurricane-force winds. Asphalt/fiber-glass shingles are very fire-resistant.	There is an asphalt roofing product for every kind of roof, from flat decks built up with building paper, tar, and gravel to sloped roofs that use asphalt rolls or shingles.	Although an asphalt shingling job could be handled by a well-instructed homeowner, you might prefer to hire a professional.	Inexpensive to moderate.
20-50 years, depending on how carefully the roof is maintained. Leaves or other debris should not be permitted to collect and gather moisture. Also, a mildewcide should be applied to shingles every 5 years.	Roofs with moderate to steep pitches.	Nailed in place over 15-pound building felt, cedar roofing can be homeowner- or professionally installed.	Moderate to expensive.
Both tile and slate are very fire-resistant, but they are also brittle. A tile or slate roof may well last 50 years or more, but individual tiles or slates are likely to need repairing periodically.	Steeply sloped roofs only.	Both clay tile and slate should be professionally installed over a strong reinforced roof and overlapping layers of 30-pound building felt.	Expensive.
Fire-resistant but subject to damage from heavy wind-blown objects. Aluminum roofs can last up to 35 years, copper and alloys even longer.	Suitable for most sloped roofs, with a few types also acceptable for flat roofs.	Can be homeowner- or professionally installed over 15-pound building felt and a normal roof support system.	Moderate.

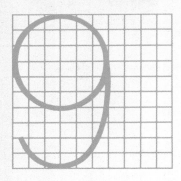

PRACTICAL
MATTERS

It's easy to daydream for hours about all the wonderful things an addition will do for your house. It's harder work—yet still fun— to develop a plan and envision how work will proceed. But before you commit yourself to a course of action, you need to evaluate costs, figure out how to finance the deal, dig into certain aspects of real estate law, and then look for and find skilled people to do the work. Unexciting assignments? Maybe so, but they're the real stuff dreams are made of.

ESTIMATING COSTS AND FINDING THE MONEY

When you plan an addition, making sense of money matters usually depends on what you intend to add, where you live, and how successful you are at shopping for the right deal. This means you need to know what your project will cost and where you can get the funds for it. What follows is generally accepted, time-tested advice about these key matters. To complete the picture, you'll have to do some additional research on your own to ascertain local conditions and current economic trends.

Tracking costs

First, the bad news. Adding on is almost always more expensive than including the same room or rooms in the original design of your home. Not only must you pay for the plans and construction, but you also may have to shell out for structural changes that will enable the addition to fit properly onto the rest of the house.

At the same time, building materials for home-improvement projects are ordinarily more expensive than those used in new-home construction. Contractors can buy materials for an entire home at bigger discounts, thanks to the greater volume involved. And, of course, inflation will, under most circumstances, make today's decision more costly than yesterday's, even if the other factors stay the same.

Labor vs. materials

You'll find that labor costs are fairly stable within a certain locale, subject only to seasonal variations. They do, however, tend to follow a specific area's cost-of-living profile. Where the cost of living is high, labor costs also will be high. In those parts of the country where living is less expensive,

labor costs will be correspondingly lower.

On the other hand, the cost of materials is often extremely volatile, shaped by supply and demand, the overall state of the economy, and many other considerations.

Before you begin the formal process of soliciting bids (see pages 138 and 139), you can learn how much to allocate for labor and materials by checking two valuable sources.

• *Appraisers.* If any organizations have to keep a close eye on construction costs, it's the lending institutions. An appraiser from a local bank or savings and loan should be able to talk to you knowledgeably about residential building costs per square foot. During the discussion, try to make direct comparisons between similar houses in the area and your plans for your house.

• *Dodge Manual.* Contractors use this handy but hefty reference as a guide to pricing and scheduling, and you can, too. (Check your local library for a copy.) Don't be put off by the avalanche of numbers and abbreviations. If you study the figures patiently, they'll yield a gold mine of information. A standard entry, for example, lists a type of building material, the amount an average worker can install in an eight-hour day, material and labor costs, and the total cost per unit.

Generally, you'll discover that the bigger, more conventional, and less mechanically complicated an addition is, the lower the cost per square foot. Smaller areas with special design touches and extensive plumbing and heating runs will be relatively more costly.

Keep in mind, though, that any figures you arrive at now are only roughly comparable. An addition built at $25 per square foot is not better than a

similar design built at $40 if it
begins to fall apart after a year
or two. In the end, the *quality*
of labor and materials makes
the difference.

Finding funds

If you have abundant cash
available and are not concerned about major expenses
in the foreseeable future—
education, vacations, and so
forth—you may choose to pay
for an addition with your own,
unborrowed funds. Of course,
if the amount you intend to
spend is already working at a
higher rate of interest than you
might be able to negotiate with
a lender, it's often wise to take
out a loan anyway.

Most people don't have this
choice. For them, building
means borrowing. The following pages tell about the most
likely sources for remodeling
money.   *(continued)*

ESTIMATING COSTS AND FINDING THE MONEY
(continued)

Yo can look to several sources of money for home-improvement projects. Because lending practices, customs, and laws vary, use this information, along with the comparisons in the chart *opposite,* as starting points in your search. Then check local conditions.

• *A conventional loan.* Commercial banks and savings and loan associations (S&Ls) are leading sources of money for home improvers. If your credit is good and your project is sound, you should have few problems getting a loan, repayable over a three- to ten-year period. Generally, the larger the loan, the longer the period of repayment and the higher the interest rate. How large a loan you can obtain depends on many factors, including your credit-worthiness, the amount of equity in your house, and the nature of the improvement project. Above a certain sum—perhaps $5,000—the lender will probably want a deed of trust—really a second mortgage—on the house as security.

Credit unions, once an abundant source of inexpensive loans, have begun to act more and more like traditional lenders, with rates no lower than those available at a bank or S&L.

• *A government-backed loan.* The most widely used is the Federal Housing Administration Title I loan, which provides for the FHA to guarantee 90 percent of the value of a loan up to $15,000, with a term of up to 15 years. The FHA charges the lender a premium of 0.5 percent and sets a ceiling on the interest rate a lender can charge. The ceiling has been about 5 percentage points above the prime rate in the past few years. You may be able to make a conventional loan at a lower rate. In communities with community development block grants, however, families meeting certain income and other conditions may be able to obtain a subsidized Title I loan with a below-market interest rate. Because of regulations and red tape, not all lenders handle Title I loans.

• *A refinanced mortgage.* You can replace the first mortgage on your house with a larger one that will give you enough cash for your improvement project. Most houses with loans that are more than ten years old have built up a large amount of equity for their owners. All you have to do to get a refinanced mortgage is prove your ability to carry a larger loan with a higher rate of interest. This increased rate is just one way you'll pay more for refinancing, however. Another is higher closing costs for the loan. Many banks and S&Ls charge 2 percent or more of the loan principal up front to settle a new loan. This means the costs of settlement—including a title search, recording and legal fees, taxes, and perhaps a new appraisal of the house—will add up to four figures, perhaps ten times the closing costs on a Title I loan.

• *A second mortgage.* Mortgage lenders and consumer finance companies have long handled this business, but, as noted above, banks and S&Ls are making more second mortgage loans these days. A second mortgage, like a refinanced mortgage, allows you to borrow against your home's unrealized equity. In this case, however, the first mortgage remains untouched. Because the lender takes a bigger risk, interest rates are usually at least two percentage points higher than on first mortgages. (Most states have recently liberalized the interest rates that non-federally regulated companies may charge.)

It's complicated to compare the costs of refinancing versus taking out a second mortgage. A new mortgage means a 20- to 30-year loan; a second mortgage will likely be paid off in five to ten years, at far less overall interest than a refinanced first mortgage; settlement costs are also lower. Most of the cost of a new long-term loan is interest, which is deductible on your income tax return. If interest rates have declined since you bought your house, refinancing could save you money, but few houses financed at levels higher than those current today have appreciated enough to give their owners much equity.

• *A life insurance loan.* Perhaps the simplest way to get money—no questions asked—is to borrow against the cash value of a life insurance policy. You can take out up to 95 percent of that figure and return it over a negotiated time—or not at all—at an attractively low interest rate (usually between 5 and 8 percent). Nonetheless, the face value will decline by the amount of the loan outstanding (although it's restored as you pay the money back).

• *A credit card loan.* For small jobs this is a distinct possibility, but watch out. Many states have raised the interest ceiling or removed it entirely. If you can pay off the loan in a relatively short time, the interest of perhaps 2 percent a month won't matter. But you may be inconvenienced by not having this borrowing power in your card for a while.

• *A personal loan.* If a family member or friend offers to help you pay for your addition, consider accepting. An interest-free loan is not as simple as it sounds, however. The person lending you money is giving up a chance to earn interest on the money elsewhere, and the IRS imputes an interest value for such loans; legally the interest is regarded as a gift. For the sake of friendship and the tax man, as well as your own records, put the terms in writing.

Be prepared
Borrowing against an insurance policy or taking out a relatively small conventional loan usually requires little paperwork. Generally, you can get the funds in a matter of days. Other sources of financing, however, demand that you present a well-thought-out set of facts to the lender. Individual institutions may request extra information; most will want to see detailed job specifications, descriptions carrying the approval of a licensed engineer, contractor, or architect. Similarly, you'll have to bring along plans that outline each and every change.

A lender also will ask to evaluate precise bids (the cost of labor and materials for the entire job) from a contractor or subcontractors. Sometimes the loan is extended directly to the contractor, who is paid on completion of the job. In this case, the contractor has obtained his own temporary financing elsewhere.

DEALING FOR DOLLARS— THE MOST LIKELY SOURCES

	ADVANTAGES	DISADVANTAGES	COMMENTS
CONVENTIONAL LOAN	For reasonably small amounts—under $10,000—this is a good choice, especially if you plan to do some of the work yourself.	Personal assets, generally your home, are required as security for amounts over $5,000.	If your credit is good and financial standing solid, a bank, S&L, or credit union should be happy to do business with you.
GOVERNMENT-BACKED LOAN	The Federal Housing Administration Title I program is a ready source of money for home improvement projects. Most applicants are eligible, suitably large sums are available, and interest rates are controlled by the FHA.	Occasionally there's burdensome red tape to contend with, and most lenders won't bother with Title I loans, particularly when interest rates are high.	You arrange the loan, which is insured by the federal government, through a bank or S&L. The government regulates the terms.
HOME-EQUITY LOAN	Both refinanced mortgages and second mortgages allow you to tap the equity in your home. A second mortgage leaves the first one intact and usually involves no prepayment penalties. Refinancing gives you the chance to negotiate a lower overall rate.	Refinancing may mean stiff new closing costs and is usually not advisable when your original mortgage has a relatively low interest rate. Second mortgages carry rates over the market level and make total payments to principal and interest very high for a time.	Some lending institutions won't make second mortgage loans or refinance first mortgages unless they sense a definite economic advantage, which may or may not be the same for you. Consumer finance companies do a lot of business in second mortgages—often at premium rates.
LIFE INSURANCE LOAN	This easy-to-get loan against a cash value carries an exceptionally low interest rate.	The policy's face value—your total coverage—decreases by the amount you borrow.	Some policies permit you to keep all coverage in place by using annual dividends to buy renewable term insurance equal to the loan amount.
CREDIT CARD LOAN	Easy to get.	High interest and loss of borrowing power until loan is repaid.	Because of their convenience, these loans are good for small projects or short periods.

DEALING WITH LEGAL AND LONG-TERM FINANCIAL MATTERS

It seems simple enough. Your land and house are, well, *yours*. You should be able to add on whatever you want, wherever you want, in any way you choose. Right? Wrong. In most parts of the country, zoning ordinances and building codes play a large role in shaping what you can and can't do—regulating everything from the height and placement of an addition to the kind of materials used to build it. And even when all the rules are followed and the work is done, you'll still have two more things to think about: higher property taxes and higher insurance premiums.

Zoning ordinances regulate what and where you can build, and, to a certain extent, how you can use your addition once it's finished. To a homeowner, effective zoning, which tightly separates residential, commercial, and industrial areas, has one important economic effect: It tends to preserve property values.

Technically, zoning applies to the ways in which *land* is used. As a practical matter, it governs the position and exterior of every *structure* within a specific area. In residential communities, ordinances usually regulate the height of buildings, their essential architectural features, and the distances they stand from property lines. Some ordinances also determine the number of nonfamily members who can live on the property and the kinds of businesses that can be operated out of a home.

Zoning guides

For a home improver, adding on means having a surveyor pinpoint where on your lot you can or can't build. Check with the local zoning or planning commission, the board of supervisors, or the building department. You'll discover that most ordinances deal with the following:

• *Size of the house*. In many cases, a residence can take up no more than 25 to 50 percent of the property it occupies.

• *Side-yard restrictions*. Nearly every set of ordinances has something to say about the distance—often a minimum of 5 feet—between your house and the neighbors' property lines.

• *Setback restrictions*. One reason why it's frequently so difficult to add on to the front of a house: Ordinances gener-

ally require that structures be ''set back'' a specified distance from the street. And in many communities, public property does *not* begin with the sidewalk; it may extend several feet onto your lot.

• *Height restrictions*. If you're adding up, the sky isn't necessarily the limit. Most ordinances restrict the height of residential buildings as measured, ordinarily, from the roof crest to the ground.

Further, some communities mandate that no house contain over a given number of square feet, a requirement that also may affect your plans. Some stipulate as well that you provide covered, off-the-street parking facilities. If you're transforming a garage into extra living space, for instance, you may have to build a covering for your car.

It's not unusual to find a particular ordinance standing in the way of the design that you think will work best for you. If so, don't automatically give up. You still may be able to build what you want, where you want (see page 137).

Easements

These also may affect the position of your addition. Easements are legal rights someone has to use part of your property for a specific purpose. Often they're granted to util-

ity companies, which periodically need to work on subterranean utility and gas lines or water mains. Easements that allow access to a particular place, by way of a driveway or road, are also common.

Whatever you do, don't take an easement lightly; you may be in for a hard fall. For example, if part of an addition blocks your neighbor's access to his home—access an easement expressly permits him to use—you may be ordered to dismantle part or all of the structure—a terribly expensive (but entirely legal) result of your failure to follow the rules.

Generally, you'll find a description of any easements in the deed to your property. But

keep in mind that easements don't necessarily have to be written down. When someone has continually and openly traveled across a portion of your property for a certain length of time (it varies from state to state), he may have established an easement "by prescription," a right most courts recognize. If you think a precedent has been established with your property, the best advice is to consult an experienced real estate lawyer.

Codes

Zoning ordinances and easements help determine *where* you can build, but a raft of highly detailed *codes*—building, plumbing, mechanical, and electrical—go a long way toward defining *how* you can build. Codes differ from state to state and even from community to community. By requiring certain methods of construction, forbidding the use of unsafe or inadequate materials, specifying who can and can't do the work (in some places, a few jobs must be left to licensed tradesmen), and setting standards of workmanship, codes safeguard not only the lives and property of individual homeowners, but the entire community as well.

Which isn't to say that some codes aren't at least partly unreasonable. Dated by the development of new methods and building materials, they may make your project more costly than it needs to be.

At the same time, some communities require that if you add on in accordance with the present codes, you must bring the rest of your house "up to code," if it isn't already. In an older home, these changes can be very expensive.

Fortunately, many codes aren't inflexible. Using a careful, thorough approach, you may be able to bypass restrictive regulations and build an addition your way (see page 137).

Experienced pros should be familiar with all local codes. When you're seeking initial estimates (see pages 138 and 139), each contractor should base his numbers on doing the job according to the regulations. If you plan to serve as your own contractor or do at least part of the work yourself (see pages 140 and 141), first get a copy of the codes and study it carefully. Then gather up your rough plans and a list of materials and contact the community's building department. The inspector there should be able to give you helpful advice about complying with each code.

The next step is to apply for a building permit. A contractor will do this for you and pay the required fee. If you're working on your own, you'll probably have to fill out an application detailing the proposed change and the estimated cost.

Often, at this stage, you'll also have to provide a fully worked detailed set of plans and specifications. Remember, however, that even if you've hired a contractor to handle these assignments, you're still responsible for making sure he has secured a permit.

Most building codes call for several mandatory inspections. Usually, the inspector will make three trips to the site: one to check the foundation, one to inspect the framing, and one to give final approval when the project is completed. If extra checks are necessary, the inspector should inform you or your contractor as the work progresses.

When he's satisfied everything is up to code, the inspector will issue a Certificate of Occupancy. This document is your legal OK to move in.

(continued)

DEALING WITH LEGAL AND LONG-TERM FINANCIAL MATTERS

(continued)

A few people take one look at the codes, do a little math on paper, and then figure they can save on labor, materials, and fees—and maybe even keep their addition hidden from the tax assessor—by simply ignoring the rules and not getting a building permit.

It's true that additions built rigidly according to code tend to be slightly *over*built: They may be a bit more sturdy and durable than is actually necessary for safety. Nevertheless, in most cases, it's a margin you shouldn't trifle with.

Further, many communities punish violators severely. Building inspectors often wield considerable authority when it comes to evaluating construction work and interpreting the codes. If you start the project before securing a permit, you may wind up paying double fees and a fine or two. If you manage to complete the job without the building department's knowing about it and then get caught later on, you may be subject to stiffer fines and even face a lawsuit. Most painfully, perhaps, you could be required to tear down the structure and begin again—if you can afford it—this time following the proper procedures.

The best advice, then, is to play within the rules. If you're thoroughly convinced that some part of the project can be done equally well using another method or material, don't just plow forward without consulting local officials. Take your case to them, work with them, and you may get the approval you're after (see the box *opposite*).

Taxing matters

One pleasant benefit of a well-conceived improvement project comes right down to the bottom line: If done right, it will most likely increase the market value of your home. The unpleasant corollary to this is that in nearly every instance, it also will increase your real estate taxes.

In certain areas, you may be able to obtain tax relief for a period of time, especially in neighborhoods where property values have plummeted and community officials see an economic advantage to letting rehabbers do their work without extra tax burdens. For the most part, however, changes that increase living space, modernize your home's interior, or add permanent structures to your yard will result in higher taxes.

Tax assessors, you'll discover, are watchful people. It's hard to hide improvements from them. When they're dealing with money matters, government personnel usually cooperate so closely it becomes almost impossible to keep your addition off the tax rolls, even if you wanted to. Specifically, the information you put down on an application for a building permit—including the project's estimated cost—goes directly from the building department to the assessor's office.

That cost estimate is critically important because the assessor will use it to help determine the value of your addition and, consequently, the reassessed value of your entire house. (Knowing this should be another good reason to limit expensive accoutrements and reduce the overall cost of the project as much as possible.)

If you plan to hire a contractor, estimates will include labor. If you're working on your own in whole or in part, the figures should, of course, be relatively lower. Will your taxes be reduced, as a result? Usually not. In most locales, the assessor will assign a certain value to your labor, add it to the cost of materials, and use the total figure to reassess your property. You'll save when you're building but not, unfortunately, when you're paying taxes.

This entire process is not so glumly cut-and-dried as it seems. Different communities assess identical improvements in different ways. In fact, individual assessors within the *same* community may arrive at slightly different values for a single project. To find out how your improvement may affect future assessments, check with a local assessor *before* you make final plans and start building. He'll probably be able to suggest acceptable alternatives that won't unduly increase your assessment.

While you're in the office, inspect the records to see how your property has been assessed in the past. Then make comparisons to your neighbors' assessments and to similar houses in the area. (These are all public documents; they should be readily available to you.)

You may discover that your property has, in fact, been overassessed, with taxes figured on a faulty description of your house and lot. Although you can't do much about the *rate* of taxation—except, perhaps, get into politics—you can appeal *assessed valuation*. The appeals process is usually not difficult, and despite what many homeowners may think, many appeals are at least partially successful. If yours is, your current taxes will be lowered, the record set straight, and a fairer basis established for future assessments.

Insurance policy

Reevaluating your homeowner's insurance is one step you can't afford to miss. Though you're likely to have adequate coverage before the project begins, you most certainly won't *after* it's completed. And if you're underinsured, your loss is likely to be greater than if you hadn't built on in the first place.

Don't wait, however, until the last nail has been driven and the family is moving in. When you have a good idea what improvements you're going to make—and well before the actual job starts—contact your agent and discuss what you have in mind. Mention how much you expect to spend, when the work is slated to begin, and when all construction should be finished. He can then boost your coverage as the work goes along. Firming up your insurance in stages will protect your investment in case the addition is damaged, or even destroyed, while it's being built.

When you talk to an agent, ask about any liability you might have while work is in progress. Reputable general contractors usually are bonded; subcontractors may or may not have adequate coverage.

In any event, this is an excellent time to shop around for new insurance. Policies and premiums vary considerably; you may be able to find equally good, maybe better, coverage at a lower cost.

Value added

To a significant extent, your home's value is set by the average value of other houses in the neighborhood. If they're selling for around $100,000, then yours is probably worth within $20,000 or so either way.

If your home is at or above the going level, it may be wise *not* to invest large sums on remodeling, unless, of course, you plan to stay put for a long time. Houses "loaded" with the latest improvements don't sell well in neighborhoods where other homes are priced considerably lower. When they can afford them, people generally like to buy expensive homes in locations where everyone else is enjoying similar luxuries.

A notable exception occurs in the kind of area mentioned earlier, where urban explorers are buying up deteriorated houses at exceptionally low prices, improving them extensively, and then watching the value of their investments skyrocket. Although the risk is relatively large—similar rehabilitations must be either planned or in progress—these investors often can sell their homes profitably later on for sums well above the purchase price and cost of improvements combined.

Nonetheless, most people aren't so adventurous. For them, the improvements that usually pay off the most in extra value are those you might expect: kitchen, bath, bedroom (no more than a total of three, however), garage, air conditioning, and family room. In most cases, they'll return at least 50 percent of your initial investment when you decide to sell; often, the yield is 75 percent or more. The exact return depends greatly on how well the work is done, how it relates to the rest of the house, and how the improved home compares in price and facilities to others in the neighborhood.

EXCEPTIONS TO THE RULES

Like all good rules, the best zoning ordinances and building codes allow for reasonable exceptions. The key word is "reasonable." In most areas, zoning and codes are matters of community concern; getting them waived is usually not as easy as changing your order in a restaurant. You'll have to arrange your arguments carefully and present them thoroughly (and for zoning changes, almost always in public). If you've hired an architect, he should be familiar with local procedures and be able to give you sound advice on how to prepare your case.

Variances
A *variance,* in effect, is public approval to go ahead with your plans, even though they're at odds with one or more of the zoning ordinances.

The process of gaining one differs from city to city and town to town. As a rule, you first fill out an application, which you get from the building department or planning board. Marshal your arguments carefully at this stage. What you need to do is show local officials that following an ordinance to the letter will cause substantial—and expensive—problems.

A petition that asks for only minor deviations from the ordinance may sail through and be approved quickly. You'll be granted what most communities call an "administrative variance." If you're requesting major

changes, your petition will be scrupulously reviewed by a group of experts.

As part of a public hearing held by the zoning commission or planning board, your request will be discussed. All interested parties—in this case, they're likely to be neighbors—will have an opportunity to give their opinions, along with expert assessments, if there are any. Afterward, your petition will be either approved or denied. If you get an OK, the variance is generally good for one year.

If your request is turned down, an appeal is possible. In most communities, you'll direct it to the city council or other legislative body, asking for a public hearing before its members. If you *still* lose out, you may be able to appeal the appeal, but at this point, you'll probably have to go to court—and that's often more costly and troublesome than it would be to absorb the blow and revise your plans.

Code changes
So you want to build *your* way, using methods and materials not covered by the local code? If you're willing to do the homework, you just might be able to.

Before you do anything else, get a copy of the code, read it completely, and make sure you understand its provisions and definitions. (Don't expect to flip through it in a matter of minutes. Unless you're nearly an expert yourself, you'll need the help of an architect or engineer.)

As you study it, you'll notice three important sections.

The first concerns *alternatives* to the code's stipulations. Look closely, and you'll see that it contains a qualifying statement saying that the code's requirements are not meant to prohibit the use of other methods, so long as they're *equivalent* to those described in the code.

This is your cue. Take your case to the building department. But before you go, be prepared. Gather supporting statements from an architect or engineer, demonstrate how other codes allow what you're proposing, even point out construction in the area that adds validity to your arguments.

If you're persuasive enough, the second significant section of the code, which gives the inspector authority to approve changes he deems acceptable, provides the building department with a full legal justification to grant your request.

If you're unsuccessful, the third section of the code is equally important. It describes in detail what you'll need to do to make formal appeal of an inspector's ruling.

PRACTICAL MATTERS

WORKING WITH A CONTRACTOR

Help! The best-laid plans can take you only so far. In most cases, you'll have to depend on a number of people—people who will do the job with expert care, on time, at a fair price, and without major complications. Often that means relying on a general contractor and a group of subcontractors employed by him. Here's what you need to know to get the job done right.

Nowadays, although many once-timid owners are picking up hammer and saw and doing at least part of the job themselves, hiring a contractor is still the most efficient way to add on. If you don't have the time, temperament, or skills to ensure that what you planned is what you get, a contractor can do it for you.

Open bidding

Start looking by soliciting recommendations from neighbors, friends, relatives, co-workers, and lending institutions. If you see a project under way in your area, stop by and take a look at it. (The box on the opposite page tells how to evaluate craftsmanship.) If all else fails, check local newspaper and Yellow Pages advertisements. Select several likely candidates, get bids from each, and then make your choice, following these steps.

• *Get rough estimates.* It's not necessary to do any further checking just yet. When you have four or five candidates, sit down with each, describe what you're after using your plan as a guide, and ask for *rough* estimates. Reliable contractors—who can't possibly cost out materials and labor at this point—will *only* give you a range of figures. Their final bids may, in fact, be slightly higher or lower. While you're talking, take the opportunity to ask for advice and suggestions. Contractors won't push possible business out the door—unless the job is very small or they're very busy—by refusing to give you a few tips.

• *Checkpoints.* Now's the time to do some detective work, and it pays to be thorough. For each contractor on your list, consider the following questions: Is he in good shape financially? Is his credit standing solid? How long has he been in business? Does he have experience doing the kind of job you're planning? Does he maintain good working relationships with subcontractors and suppliers (meaning, often, does he pay them on schedule)? Is he bonded, insured against property damage, and covered by workmen's compensation? Is he personable—that is, will you be able to work comfortably with him? The same sources who gave you the original recommendations also should be able to answer these questions. Finally, don't neglect the most likely source of all: the contractor himself. Ask for references—any reputable businessman will honor the request. Talk to homeowners he's worked for and then critically inspect the results.

• *Bidding.* Get final bids from no fewer than three contractors. Submit your working plans and go over them with every bidder. Specify the quality of materials you're seeking, and note the brands, patterns, or model numbers of products. Precision is mandatory. Each candidate must use exactly the same information; otherwise, the figures won't be comparable. Request the bids by a certain date (three weeks to review specifications should be enough), and when they're in, evaluate each one with the contractor who submitted it.

• *Pick one.* Exceptionally low bids may be appealing, but they often mean you'll receive inferior materials and bad workmanship. Very high bids may indicate the best of everything (which you may or may not want), but they also could reflect a lot of overhead or abnormally high profit margins. Other things being equal, the one in the middle is usually the most acceptable choice.

Sign here

Once you've made a selection, don't relax—you're not home free yet. The next step is to legally seal the deal with a binding contract. Keep these points in mind before signing.

Straight talk is all-important. The contract should *clearly* describe every part of the job: a starting date, precise specifications, a guarantee covering the work for three to five years, a schedule of payments, and a completion date. To show your concern for getting things done without too much delay, this last section should include the phrase *time is of the essence.* The document also should require the contractor to go about his business *in a workmanlike manner*, meaning simply—but significantly—that he must do the work correctly.

Money talks, too, and you've got it on your side. Some contractors may ask for a substantial down payment (50 percent or more) before the work even begins. Don't agree to this. (Most lending institutions won't allow you to anyway; to protect their interests, they'll only pay out when work is under way and as it progresses.)

A commonly used method of payment written into many contracts calls for one-third when you sign, another third when the job is half completed, and the final third when the entire project is finished. It's often a good idea to insert a clause into the contract that allows you to withhold at least part of the final payment for a minimum of 30 days. During this time, you can see for yourself if the work was done properly and—because you still have the contractor's money in your pocket—require fine-tuning, if necessary.

Few projects proceed exactly as you, or the contractor, expected. You or he may sug-

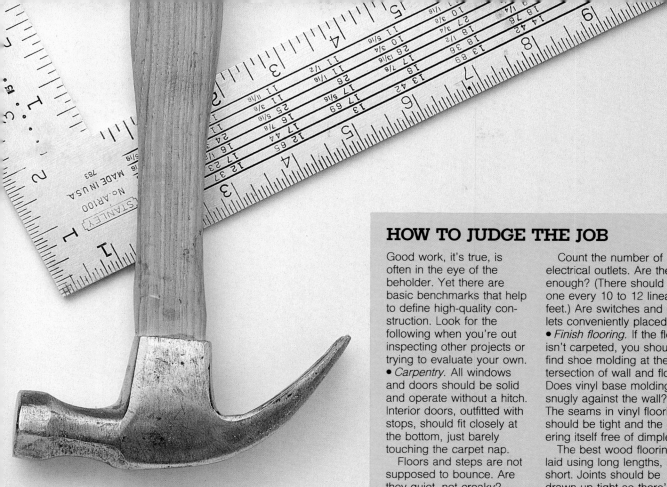

gest a different way of doing things. Simply make sure to add a description of the change and its cost to the contract before going ahead.

Who's responsible?

In most cases, and in most places, a contractor has a standard set of duties. He schedules and supervises the entire job. He orders and pays for all building supplies, seeing that they're shipped to the site as needed. He hires and pays a group of subcontractors—excavators, carpenters, plumbers, electricians, and so forth—and coordinates their work so the project goes smoothly and efficiently. He also oversees the budget and periodically inspects the work himself to ensure that it's being done carefully and correctly.

Your role at this stage should be relatively passive. If, in your opinion, part of the job isn't up to snuff, resist talking to the subcontractors about it: They're not working for you. Take your complaints or suggestions directly to the contractor or your architect. (For more about working

with an architect, see pages 64-71.)

Beyond serving as a coordinator, paymaster, and on-site inspector, a contractor has other tasks related to the job. He must get and pay for all building permits, utility connection fees, and licenses (and, by extension, is required to comply with local ordinances and codes). He's also responsible for alerting the building department when it's time for inspections and for leaving the room or rooms clean enough to occupy once the work is done (adding "broom clean" to a description of the project in the contract will do the trick).

And one more thing

Your search will probably turn up an honest and excellent workman. Nonetheless, for your protection, here's another consideration to nail down. To avoid unpaid bills and maybe one or more liens against your property, ask the contractor to have each supplier and subcontractor (as well as himself) sign a document called a "waiver of liens" before you make the final payment.

HOW TO JUDGE THE JOB

Good work, it's true, is often in the eye of the beholder. Yet there are basic benchmarks that help to define high-quality construction. Look for the following when you're out inspecting other projects or trying to evaluate your own.
• *Carpentry.* All windows and doors should be solid and operate without a hitch. Interior doors, outfitted with stops, should fit closely at the bottom, just barely touching the carpet nap.

Floors and steps are not supposed to bounce. Are they quiet, not creaky?

Can you see nail "pops" through the drywall? Are seams overly apparent, particularly at night?

Trim work should be sanded and joints securely mitered. Inspect wood molding for precise, careful seaming.

Do an air check. Can you feel drafts near windows and doors? Along joints where the floor and wall and ceiling and wall meet?

Are bookshelves and closet hanging rods properly bracketed? You should find brackets every 4 feet on bookshelves and every 5 feet on rods. Kitchen cabinets should be screwed to the wall, not nailed.
• *Working parts.* Is the toilet tight, or does it wobble? The tub should be adequately caulked, the shower head securely positioned, and ceramic tile, if any, sufficiently grouted. Are faucets on straight?

Count the number of electrical outlets. Are there enough? (There should be one every 10 to 12 linear feet.) Are switches and outlets conveniently placed?
• *Finish flooring.* If the floor isn't carpeted, you should find shoe molding at the intersection of wall and floor. Does vinyl base molding fit snugly against the wall? The seams in vinyl flooring should be tight and the covering itself free of dimples.

The best wood flooring is laid using long lengths, not short. Joints should be drawn up tight so there's little space between boards.

If carpeting is the floor covering, it should be stretched tightly, with no noticeable seams or piecing.
• *Outside.* For proper drainage, the grade must slope away from the house. In addition, splashblocks should be placed near downspouts to move rainwater away from the structure.

Has brick or other kinds of masonry been "washed down?" In other words, has excess mortar been cleared away and its residue cleaned off?

Check the caulking around windows and doors. Is it smooth and unbroken?

SERVING AS YOUR OWN CONTRACTOR

Very few homeowners have the time, stamina, or inclination to construct an entire addition solo—but this doesn't necessarily mean you must surrender responsibility and control. You might choose to serve as your own general contractor, lining up subs and supervising their efforts. You could even take on some parts of the job yourself. But first, carefully consider what's involved in doing your own contracting.

Serving as your own contractor usually saves money, but do you really want the job? To find out, ask yourself these questions.
• Do you have both the time and the patience to schedule and supervise a series of complex operations?
• Are you knowledgeable about construction? If not, are you willing to study and learn?
• Will you save more money than you could earn (after taxes) by applying the same time and effort to your regular work?
• Do you have the assertiveness to oversee workers and question them if necessary?
• Can you stay cool in the heat of inevitable emergencies?
• Are you a reasonably skilled do-it-yourselfer?

Unless you can answer yes to at least a majority of these questions, you should probably let a professional contractor take care of business.

Even if you do decide to award the bid to yourself, bear in mind that being the boss means just that. *You'll* have to hire and pay subcontractors. *You'll* have to coordinate their efforts and schedule the job. *You'll* have to apply for building permits and summon local inspectors. And, without a doubt, you'll need the tact to resolve disputes, along with the gumption to get your way, if necessary.

Without putting it into so many words, you may have served as your own contractor on smaller projects—a new kitchen or bath, for example. Neither assignment is easy by any means, but each involves supervising no more than four or five subcontractors (plumber, electrician, cabinet and counter-top installer, and maybe a carpenter and painter).

Major jobs, such as adding a new wing, often call for as many as 10 to 15 subcontractors to handle the myriad steps in the building process—excavation, masonry, heating and air conditioning, flooring, roofing, painting, plumbing, electrical work, carpentry, and so forth.

Hiring help
Whatever the size of the project and the number of subs you have to employ, there's a reasonable path to follow when you're running the whole show yourself. Unsurprisingly, it's much like the one you'd take to hire a general contractor.

Make sure all plans and specifications are in writing and are thoroughly detailed. If you're using an architect, he may take care of this step (see pages 64-71). If you're not, it may still be worthwhile to have a pro do the basic plans and specifications, especially for a large or complicated job. You'll save by doing the architect's supervisory work yourself.

Search for reliable subcontractors. Solicit recommendations, check references, and carefully inspect past work, paying special attention to projects done by the main subcontractors you're likely to hire (carpenters, plumbers, and electricians). Although general contractors should have heavy-duty experience, don't automatically reject a novice sub. You may find a competent person just getting started who's willing to charge a little less to build up business. Conversely, don't immediately jump at the lowest bid.

Particularly if a job is out of the ordinary, spending slightly more for a highly skilled and experienced worker may often be worth the extra money.

Check work habits. No matter how skilled they are at their trade, some subcontractors are inconveniently independent people: They follow no clock but their own. More often, subs get overextended or underestimate how long work will take—yours or someone else's. Also, they're affected by delays from other subs and have difficulty juggling jobs. Just one slow-motion worker can add days or even weeks to the project. Obviously, checking work habits before hiring anyone is a good idea, and the contract is always a powerful ally. Nevertheless, *you* must make sure that each part of the overall job is done to your satisfaction *on time*. If you can't supervise adequately, pay one of the subs a little extra to oversee the project when you're not there. The master carpenter, whose work usually overlaps a number of stages, is often the best choice.

When you're discussing payment, you'll discover that subcontractors like to work in one of two ways. Some prefer to give you a package price for the entire job; others work on a "time and materials" basis—you pay so much per hour, plus the cost of materials. A package price lets you more accurately forecast what you'll be spending. If a worker insists on being paid by the hour, suggest an upper limit.

Sign a contract with each and every sub, following the suggestions outlined on pages 138 and 139. Make sure each subcontractor has workers' compensation and liability insurance. Ask for certificates.

Getting organized

Contact your community's building department and review your plans with the local inspector, who will tell you which permits you need and when inspections are necessary. He also should be able to give you directions on how to comply with codes and ordinances. *Don't* take any shortcuts at this point. Building inspectors usually have absolute authority to order work dismantled if it's done incorrectly without a permit.

The trickiest part of contracting is scheduling and supervising the work. With some exceptions, each sub's job is dependent on the others', which means that one stage of the project has to be completed before another can begin. Your task is to arrange the work flow so subs are coming and going but never coming and just standing around.

When each subcontractor's work is concluded, ask for a waiver of liens, together with receipts showing that he's paid all suppliers. Do this before making the final payment.

Pitching in

Of course, the division of labor doesn't have to be so neat and clean. Whether you're working with a contractor or serving as your own, you may be skilled enough to handle several of the jobs a sub would ordinarily do. In many communities, however, certain tasks—like some kinds of plumbing and electrical work—are out of bounds to anyone but licensed tradesmen. You won't be able to do them no matter how talented you are.

And you may find that some professionals simply refuse to work with nonprofessional help—even their own clients'.

Nonetheless, in most cases, the opportunity exists to do as much as your time and expertise permit. Be honest, though. If you fool yourself into thinking you'll save a lot of money by doing many jobs yourself without the proper skills, you may end up with a project so badly bungled it has to be done over again—this time by a pro.

Further, poorly done remodeling can only detract from the value, function, and appearance of your home. It may even pose critical safety hazards. As in other things, then, know thyself.

Know your schedule, too. Remember that the most scrupulously planned projects, even with a contractor riding herd and an architect supervising the work, often take longer than expected. If you don't have time to supervise the job—or the stamina to see it through—get some help; otherwise, the entire project may drag on and on.

If you're not dissuaded yet, you're probably a do-it-yourselfer who can really do it. Described below are a number of jobs you should be able to tackle on your own—and a few more best left to a hired hand.

• *Excavating.* Digging for even a small foundation can take weeks of back-breaking labor. If you have the time and strength, go ahead. Generally, however, it's a better idea to hire an excavator with heavy machinery to do the same thing in a day or two.

• *Plumbing.* Believe it or not, some plumbing work is not as mystifyingly difficult as many laymen think. After reading a good instructional book or two, you can modify supply lines or add to them. Drain work, though, is a different matter. If community codes require cast-iron drainpipes, the work can be muscle-wrenching and tricky; lightweight plastic drain systems are easier for amateurs to work with, but not all codes permit them.

• *Wiring.* Actually doing the work is easier than it seems; running wires and making connections are not complicated tasks. However, laying out the entire electrical system on paper so it'll function safely is another matter. If you're not positively sure how to proceed, hire an electrician to help. If your house requires new service from the street, an electrician will do this also. *You* can install house wiring beyond the service panel.

• *Drywalling.* Here, the scope of the job should determine who does it. You can put up relatively small amounts of drywall yourself—and save money in the process. On the other hand, a contractor, working swiftly with specialized equipment and scaffolding, can sometimes buy and install large quantities of drywall for less than it would take you just to purchase the materials.

• *Painting, papering, paneling, and minor demolition.* Each of these takes only rudimentary skill. Once you have organized your materials and know how to proceed, you'll complete the work in only slightly more time than a pro would.

10

FINISHING TOUCHES

Though this chapter comes last in the book, the best finishing touches should really be part of your plan from the beginning. Skylights, kitchen and bath extras, and the other niceties covered on the pages that follow will cost less and fit in better if you include them in your original list of "wants" for an addition.

Windows to the sky can bring sunlight to unexpected spaces—at a surprisingly modest cost. The secret is to select kit-form skylights, which include a plastic bubble and most of the parts you need to install it. If you have all the materials on hand, plus the help of a friend to hoist the assembly onto the roof, you can install one in a day.

The glazing in most skylights is two panes thick to minimize heat loss in winter and hold in cool air in hot weather. Many skylights open to provide ventilation as well as light. Since skylights are usually manufactured to fit between standard rafter spacing, plan a location that lets you take advantage of this convenient feature.

The skylights shown *above* and *opposite* open directly to the rooms they are intended to benefit. If your attic separates the roof from a room you'd like to light, build a light shaft. A light shaft starts with a hole in the ceiling that lines up with the skylight; plywood encloses all four sides.

In the fieldstone shower *above*, a 36-inch-square skylight set into the tongue-and-groove ceiling washes the corner with natural light and creates a forestlike atmosphere.

The custom-designed kitchen *opposite* looks even better flooded with sunshine from banks of skylights along the ridgeline. Set on a north-south axis, they provide maximum light and minimal heat buildup during the heat of the day. A semicircular clerestory window set above the far end of the kitchen catches more sun.

KITCHEN EXTRAS

All kitchens serve the same basic functions— meal planning and preparation, storage, and cleanup. But those tasks mean different things to different people. This means, of course, that there's no such thing as *the* perfect kitchen—only the kitchen that serves you best. Specialized work spaces, lighting that brightens an often-used corner, flexible seating, even conveniently placed hooks to hang potholders and dish-cloths, are among the variables that put the finishing touches on a kitchen.

If a new kitchen will be part of the addition you're thinking about, you have an excellent opportunity to eliminate all the problems that vexed you about the old one. The three photos here abound in ideas you can adapt.

The focal point of the sleek but not overly large kitchen *above* is an unusually shaped center island that takes up little space and serves several functions. A drop-in range is the pivot of the work triangle between refrigerator and sink. An eating table, which forms a semicircle at a lower height than the cooking surface, is handy for informal meals. A triangular cabinet offers convenient storage, with a tile inset on top that's useful as a resting place for hot pots.

This imaginatively designed, compact arrangement takes up less space than a typical rectangular island. If you're planning a new or remodeled kitchen, and you like the idea of an island but don't want to sacrifice a lot of floor space, an arrangement like this might be worth considering.

Islands can be custom-built to suit your work patterns; they also can be ready-made from stock cabinets. A small island need not be stationary— mounted on casters, it can go anywhere you need it, though you'd have to give up any feature that requires electrical or gas hookups.

Island-plus

A towering stone fireplace, a large dropped fluorescent fixture, and a center island that allows for both informal eating space and a pullout worktable make the kitchen/family room *opposite, top* a practical and inviting activity center.

This double room was added to a family's home after they'd lived there several years. They knew by then what they needed in the way of space and organization. The addition has a warm, welcoming atmosphere, lots of room for group cooking and snack-making, and an abundance of useful, thoughtful details: The worktable is just the right height for kneading dough, and electrical outlets at the side of the island accommo-

date a toaster, electric mixer, and other small appliances.

Storage

One of the major reasons you're planning to add kitchen space or build a new kitchen may be a need for more storage. Lots of drawer and cabinet space isn't the only way to meet this need, though. Specialized cabinets—with interior features that include lazy Susans, vertical tray partitions, and slide-out trays for pans, for example—can help you maximize wall space so that you're not necessarily surrounded by cabinets.

The well-organized drawers and cabinet shelves *at right* incorporate ideas that can make storage in any kitchen more efficient and compact.

• A magnetic knife rack keeps knives in good order, easy to get to, safer, and sharper than if they were lying loose.

• A slide-out cutting board above the knife drawer uses space that would otherwise be wasted.

• An in-drawer spice rack, set at an angle, keeps herbs and spices handy and leaves room for small utensils as well. Array your seasonings alphabetically so you can locate the one you need quickly.

• The deep cabinet is divided into useful levels by plywood shelves. On top are space-hogging baking pans and casseroles. Below are potatoes and onions stored in plastic bins.

BATH
EXTRAS

Adding a bath to your home is a great way to get your family's day off to a faster start—and almost certainly will add to your home's resale value. But a new bath can be more than just a place to get clean. Consider making it someplace special with an oversize tub, or go a step further and treat yourself to a spa or hot tub. If space and privacy permit, you can bring in a view of the outside world—or even bathe out there.

The large greenhouse windows in the luxurious spa *opposite* provide a view over the treetops—and no corresponding view in. A standard whirlpool unit of acrylic was set into a custom-poured synthetic marble surround that includes generous ledge space for planters.

In the equally appealing retreat *above,* a bathroom wall of sliding glass patio doors shows the way to the small deck and its hot tub of laminated teak. (Hot tubs are traditionally made of redwood, but teak is an elegant alternative; other options include cedar, mahogany, and oak.) The bathing

area, carved out of a hillside, features a sculptured concrete retaining wall topped with translucent plastic panels for privacy and a dome-shape canvas roof for weather protection.

Available by mail, hot tub kits can save you about one-third of the cost of a professional hot tub installation. They're available with a variety of heating elements to make them practical in just about any climate. Once you've assembled your kit, you may want—or need—professional help with the plumbing and

wiring. Be sure to check local requirements, which vary from community to community.

If all you really want is a bath with a little extra space, charm, or practicality, think about using floor space to its greatest effect. Would side-by-side sinks, either freestanding or set in a long vanity, meet your family's needs? What about partitioning the sink area from the toilet and tub, so two people can share facilities? A heated towel bar or graceful brass bathrobe rack may be the only extra touches you need to make your new bath into a special addition.

ENTERTAINMENT CENTERS

Whether your home entertainment revolves around puzzles and games, arts and crafts, or big-screen TV and electronic challenges, you know that finding space for them can be a problem. If the addition you're thinking of includes a family room, space to store—and enjoy—your gear should head your list of must-haves. From toddlers' toys to sophisticated video equipment, your home entertainment center must take everyone in your family into account. On these pages are two solutions that work. We hope they'll help you find even more answers.

A floor-to-ceiling unit combining open shelves and closed cabinets along a whole wall isn't too much storage for most families. You may not want to feel that your family room/entertainment center is one big closet, however. A few space-saving tricks can minimize the "storage-storage-everywhere" look.

In the add-on family room *above*, the owners incorporated storage cubbies into the space below the padded window seats. Games, craft materials, and other items are accessible, but concealed and unobtrusive. Along one wall,

a bank of sleek oak cabinets holds stereo equipment, records, and a TV set mounted on a pullout shelf with a lazy Susan that lets it swivel so it can be viewed from different angles. The closed cabinets protect the electronic gear from dust and accidents and give the room a tidy air.

The projection TV in the room *opposite* could be an overpowering element if it weren't carefully incorporated into the furniture arrangement. To-the-ceiling bookcases

balance it visually, and the built-in's finish was carefully custom-matched with the TV. This entertainment center also accommodates stereo equipment.

Built-ins like those shown here are easier to install—and less expensive—if you plan ahead. If you're adding a whole new room, working storage into the design from the outset will probably save you a lot of money and effort later. If you're looking for more space but prefer not to add on, storage projects like these may be the answer.

WORK, PLANNING, AND HOBBY CENTERS

Is your kitchen table often cluttered with hobby materials, or your sewing machine rarely used because it's stuck away in a closet? If so, provide for these and other activities in your new addition. A well-organized laundry/sewing center, a place to balance the checkbook and organize menus, or table space reserved for crafts projects help any new room live bigger.

One well-planned activity center can often serve a variety of functions. Study, for example, the bountifully windowed desk-corner in the kitchen addition shown *above*.

The built-in desk fits neatly at one end of the kitchen cabinets. Adults in the family use it for budget and meal planning, children for homework and crafts. A shallow center drawer and three file-size drawers allow family members to keep materials close to the work center when it's being used by others.

Multipurpose task center

The carefully planned and organized center *at right* takes up only a corner of a family room addition, but it's compact and versatile, and plays four different roles—all well. Besides acting as a laundry and sewing room, the area also makes an ideal mud room and planting center, thanks to its

location at the rear of the house.

Perforated hardboard mounted above the sewing table provides a storage wall for thread and sewing tools, and drawers on either side of the center hold fabric and patterns.

The laundry center houses a washer, dryer, and sink (not shown). The sink is a good example of preinstallation planning: It's deep enough for hand washing and presoaking laundry, arranging flowers, and potting or spraying houseplants. The portable shelf unit near the sliding glass door serves both as a place to sort and fold clothes and as a handy carrier.

The floor is easy-care vinyl that looks like flagstone; here there's no fear of damage from muddy sneakers or the drips and spills of laundry and planting chores. (More about flooring on pages 154 and 155.)

WALLS
AND CEILINGS

Any newly painted or papered wall or ceiling will look fresh and sparkling, but to achieve the most from a new look, it must be coordinated with the room's overall decorating plan. If you envision a very dramatic or colorful decorating scheme, neutral or conservative wall and ceiling treatments may be your best choice. If, on the other hand, you want the walls and ceilings of your addition to do more, these two pages can help you make them special.

If your addition is a family room or den, you may already have thought of paneling your walls. Easy installation, durability, and warm good looks make manufactured paneling a good choice in many settings. If you're thinking of wood, here are other options to consider.

For example, in the sparkling-new eat-in kitchen *above, left*, honey-tone wood strips follow the curve of the ceiling down to the over-counter window. Strips, available in a wide variety of woods and at correspondingly varied prices, come with either square or interlocking edges in lengths up to 20 feet. Because strips are less than 1 inch thick and less than 3 inches wide, they're not especially heavy—an important consideration when you're working on a ceiling, or even trying to put up four walls' worth of wood.

Another alternative to manufactured paneling is boards, either fresh-cut from a mill or recycled from an older structure. The pale-toned rough-sawn boards in the bedroom *above, right* add rustic charm.

Applying any kind of solid-wood treatment requires more carpentry know-how than you need for putting up sheet paneling, but you get a broader choice of finish, grain, and design possibilities. For example, you can apply boards or strips vertically, horizontally, diagonally, in a board-and-batten configuration, or even in a parquet pattern.

The advantages of solid wood don't stop here. Wood helps deaden sound from room to room and does more than give your addition a warm look—it can actually help keep you warm by contributing additional insulation to walls and ceilings.

The fresh, outdoor charm of the garden room *at left* also traces its origins to wood. White latticework panels were applied over furring strips to set them off from the dark-painted walls. The panels are prebuilt, lightweight, easy to install, and moderately priced.

Other options

Wood isn't your only choice. Other appealing, non-run-of-the-mill wall and ceiling alternatives include:
• *Brick and stone veneers.* Thin slices of the real thing, veneers give you the look of their heavier counterparts but are inexpensive and easy to install.

• *Ceramic tile.* An attractive, waterproof choice for a kitchen or bathroom addition, tile is moderate to expensive in price but virtually maintenance-free.
• *Pressed metal.* Painted or left gleamingly natural, "tin" gives a brand-new room a touch of yesterday's charm. It's available in a wide variety of patterns in 2x6- and 2x8-foot panels that are moderately difficult to install.
• *Carpeting.* Provides softness and texture on walls and ceilings, and is a good sound barrier. Apply carpeting with waterproof latex adhesive; tack it in place while adhesive is drying.

153

FLOORS

For floors, many remodelers automatically think of carpeting, and maybe that's the best choice for your addition. But several alternatives—resilient tiles and sheet goods, wood, and hardsurface flooring—offer you a chance to be adventurous and experiment with colors, textures, or materials that you've never had a chance to try in the original house. Here's how these options compare.

In the sunlit new entry shown *above*, guests step onto a chessboard of vinyl tile that's durable, easy-to-maintain, affordable, and strikingly attractive.

Before this seating and greeting area was added, guests entered directly into the living room. Now the homeowners have a surface that can stand up to dripping umbrellas and muddy boots, yet requires no more upkeep than an occasional washing and waxing.

Resilient tiles and sheet goods—softer underfoot than anything but carpeting—range in price from inexpensive to moderate; most are designed for do-it-yourself installation.

The warmth of wood
Wood flooring offers durability, beauty, and lots of design versatility. In the two-level family room addition *opposite, above,* ordinary tongue-and-groove oak strips were laid diagonally and bleached. The result: an effective backdrop for colorful accessories and deep-toned walls, with dynamic lines that visually widen the space.

Other wood flooring options include random-width pine or oak planks and prefinished parquet tiles. All require periodic waxing and buffing, and none stand up to water and heavy traffic as well as resilient

and hard-surface materials. Installing wood strips and planks requires moderate carpentry skills; parquet tiles stick down as easily as their resilient cousins. Prices range from moderate (strips) to expensive (prefinished parquet tiles).

Hard-surface materials

Hard-surface floorings offer a wide range of texture and design possibilities.

• *Quarry tile* on the floor of the gracious new bedroom *at left* gets its sheen from a thin seal of acrylic wax, reapplied twice a year and simply buffed between waxings. Quarry and paver tiles—made from natural clays in 6- to 8-inch squares and 4x8-inch rectangles—are moderately priced but also moderately difficult for amateurs to install.

• *Slate* is highly stain-resistant but scuffs in heavy traffic and needs regular waxing. It's expensive and moderately difficult to install.

• *Ceramic tiles* come in myriad sizes, shapes, and colors. With ceramic tile, your design choices are almost unlimited. Cost is moderate to high, depending mainly on the tiles you select; installing ceramic tile flooring is a fairly tricky do-it-yourself task.

• *Marble* is well suited to formal, elegant settings but stains easily, requires regular waxing, is expensive, and must be professionally installed. In many homes, *terrazzo*, a man-made product consisting of marble or stone chips set in cement, is used instead. It is highly resistant to staining.

• *Brick* is a less expensive hard-surface option. Its warm color and rough texture are especially effective in rooms with a country flavor. Brick floors need occasional waxing to look their best.

155

WHERE TO GO FOR MORE INFORMATION

Better Homes and Gardens® Books
Would you like to learn more about adding on to your home? These Better Homes and Gardens® books can help.

Better Homes and Gardens®
NEW DECORATING BOOK
How to translate ideas into workable solutions for every room in your home. Choosing a style, furniture arrangements, windows, walls and ceilings, floors, lighting, and accessories. 433 color photos, 76 how-to illustrations, 432 pages.

Better Homes and Gardens®
COMPLETE GUIDE TO HOME REPAIR,
MAINTENANCE, & IMPROVEMENT
Inside your home, outside your home, your home's systems, basics you should know. Anatomy and step-by-step drawings illustrate components, tools, techniques, and finishes. 515 how-to techniques; 75 charts; 2,734 illustrations; 552 pages.

Better Homes and Gardens®
COMPLETE GUIDE TO GARDENING
A comprehensive guide for beginners and experienced gardeners. Houseplants, lawns and landscaping, trees and shrubs, greenhouses, insects and diseases. 461 color photos, 434 how-to illustrations, 37 charts, 552 pages.

Better Homes and Gardens®
STEP-BY-STEP BUILDING SERIES
A series of do-it-yourself building books that provides step-by-step illustrations and how-to information for starting and finishing many common construction projects and repair jobs around your house. More than 90 projects and 1,200 illustrations in this series of six 96-page books:
STEP-BY-STEP BASIC PLUMBING
STEP-BY-STEP BASIC WIRING
STEP-BY-STEP BASIC CARPENTRY
STEP-BY-STEP HOUSEHOLD REPAIRS
STEP-BY-STEP MASONRY & CONCRETE
STEP-BY-STEP CABINETS & SHELVES

Other Sources of Information
Many professional and special-interest associations publish catalogs, style books, or product brochures that are available upon request.

American Gas Association
1515 Wilson Blvd.
Arlington, VA 22209

American Hardboard Association (AHA)
887-B Wilmette Road
Palatine, IL 60607

American Home Lighting Institute
230 N. Michigan Avenue
Chicago, IL 60601

Association of Home Appliance Manufacturers (AHAM)
20 N. Wacker Drive
Chicago, IL 60606

Ceilings and Interior Systems Contractors Association (CISCA)
1800 Pickwick Ave.
Glenview, IL 60025

Cellulose Manufacturers Association (CMA)
5908 Columbia Pike
Baileys Crossroads, VA 22041

Exterior Insulation Manufacturers Association (EIMA)
1000 Vermont Avenue NW, Suite 1200
Washington, DC 20005

Gypsum Association
1603 Orrington Ave.
Evanston, IL 60201

Major Appliance Consumer Action Panel (MACAP)
20 N. Wacker Dr.
Chicago, IL 60606

National Association of the Remodeling Industry
11 E. 44th St.
New York, NY 10017

National Center for a Barrier-Free Environment
Suite 1006
1140 Connecticut Ave. NW
Washington, DC 20036

National Housewares Manufacturers Association (NHMA)
1130 Merchandise Mart
Chicago, IL 60654

National Kitchen and Bath Association (NKBA)
114 Main Street
Hackettstown, NJ 07840

National Trust for Historic Preservation
1785 Massachusetts Ave. NW
Washington, DC 20036

Tile Council of America
Box 326
Princeton, NJ 08540

ACKNOWLEDGMENTS

Architects and Designers

The following is a page-by-page listing of the architects, designers, builders, and space planners whose work appears in this book.

Cover:
   Nancy Elliott
Pages 12-13
   William Remick
   Judith Olsen
   Don Pederson
Pages 14-15
   Finegold and Bullis, AIA
Pages 16-17
   Jeremiah Eck, The Associated Architects
Pages 18-19
   Penny Delesdernier and Ann Brown
Pages 22-23
   Marvin Ullman, AIA
Pages 24-25
   Sandra Banks
Pages 26-27
   Mary Jo and Tom Consiglio
Pages 30-31
   Allan Grant, AIA
   Larry N. Deutsch, ASID
Pages 32-33
   Virginia Frankel, ASID
Pages 34-35
   James and Sharon Stoebner
Pages 36-37
   William Ludwig, AIA
Pages 38-39
   Peter David DiPietro
Pages 40-41
   Rusty Barber, AIA, Surber and Barber
Pages 42-43
   Barbara Epstein
Pages 44-45
   Charles Montgomery, AIA
Pages 46-47
   Stephen Guerrant, Architectural Associates
Pages 48-49
   William Remick
   Judith Oken
Pages 50-51
   Thomas M. Tebbetts, AIA
   Robert Payne Newton, ASID

Pages 52-53
   Jane Griswold
Pages 54-55
   Blair Pope
Pages 56-57
   Nancy Elliott
Pages 58-59
   Mark Hajjar
Pages 60-61
   Robert Kilgore, AIA
   McEnary, Krafft, Birch, and Kilgore, Inc.
   Laurence T. Mork, ASID
Pages 62-63
   Edward Bing and Associates
Pages 64-65
   George Hopkins, Jr., AIA
Pages 80-95
   William Ludwig, AIA
Pages 96-97
   Don Beletsky, Otis Associates
Pages 100-101
   Dean Paulson
Pages 104-105
   Stephen Mead Associates
Pages 106-107
   Perez Associates, Inc.
Pages 108-109
   Edward Bing and Associates
Pages 142-143
   W. Lamar Cheatham III
   Paden Prichard
Pages 144-145
   Howard Glickman, St. Louis Group, Inc.
   Tom Parson, Hans Hanson Importers
   Linda Joan Smith
Pages 146-147
   Kathryne Weaver
   Linda Bressler Interior Design
Pages 148-149
   Don Olsen Associates
   Corky Wolk
Pages 150-151
   Harley Jensen, AIA
Pages 152-153
   Ernst Dorfi
   Judy Rock
Pages 154-155
   Gary Owen
   Richard Taylor
   Rosanne Holliday, Del Mar Designs

Photographers and Illustrators

We extend our thanks to the following photographers and illustrators whose creative talents and technical skills contributed much to this book.

Ernest Braun
Ross Chapple
Nanci Doonan
George de Gennaro
Bob Hawks
Hedrich-Blessing
Hopkins Associates
Fred Lyon
Maris/Semel
E. Alan McGee
Frank Lotz Miller
Carson Ode
John Rogers
Jessie Walker
Sandra Williams

INDEX

ADDING ON

INDEX
(continued)

P-S

Paint
    exterior, 122, *123, 124,*
    124-125
    interior, *24-25*
Patios, *104-105*
    walk-out, for basement, *36*
Personal loans, 132
Plants, use of, *18-19*
    porch conversion, *38-39*
Playroom, dormer, *62*
Plumbing work, 90, 141
Plywood
    sheathing, *88-89*
    siding, 114, *116,* 116-117
Porches
    addition, *64,* 65
    enclosing, *38-39*
        family rooms, *6-7,* 96, *97*
    enclosing of space over, *50*
Preliminary drawings, 70, 72
Preservatives/sealers for
    siding, 122, *123, 124,*
    124-125
Professionals, use of
    contractors, 138-139
    subcontractors, 140, 141
    See also Design
        professionals, use of
Quarry tile floors, *38-39,*
    54-55, 155
Ramps, for disabled, *78*
Ranch houses, 98
    add-on options, 98, *99*
Refinanced mortgages, 132,
    133
Remodeling. *See* Adding in
Resilient flooring, *154*
Roofs
    for bay, *60*
    finishing, *92-93*
    framing, *86*
    materials, 93, *126,* 127
        chart, *128,* 128-129
    sheathing, *88-89*
Room switching, *20-21*
Rough drawings, 70
Rugs
    area, *24-25*
    woven, *20*
Sand-spray siding, 110, *112,*
    112-113
Scale, manipulating, *18-19*
    with mirrors, *19, 26-27, 37,*
    42-43

Schematic (rough) drawings,
    70
Sealers, clear, 122, *123, 124,*
    124-125
    for roofing, *126*
Seating pieces, *32-33*
    bay window and, *60-61*
    and mirror use, *26-27*
    and visual weight, *18-19*
Second mortgages, 132, 133
Semitransparent stain, use of,
    122, *123, 124,* 124-125
Sewing/laundry area, *150-151*
Sheathing work, *88-89*
Shed dormers, *63*
Shelves, built-in, *57, 59*
Shingles and rolls, asphalt,
    126, 127, *128,* 128-129
Shingles and shakes
    roofing, *126,* 127, *128,*
    128-129
    siding, 114, *116,* 116-117
Shower, fieldstone, skylight for,
    142
Siding
    finishes for, 122, *123*
        chart, *124,* 124-125
    manufactured, 110, *111*
        chart, *112,* 112-113
    natural wood, 114, *115*
        chart, *116,* 116-117
Skylights, *81, 97, 100-101,*
    142-143
Slate and tile, roofing, 127,
    128, 128-129
Slump stone, 119, *120,*
    120-121
Solar energy, use of, *76-77*
Solarium addition, *100-101*
Spa, *146*
Split-level and split-entry
    houses, 98
    add-on options, 98, *99*
Stains (finishes), 122, *123,*
    124, 124-125
Stairways
    attic, 34
    basement, opened-up, *37*
    for second-story addition,
    102
Steel and aluminum siding,
    110, *112,* 112-113
Stone as surface material,
    118, 119, *120,* 120-121
Storage
    bedroom, *22-23, 30-31*
    for bedroom expansion, 50

Storage *(contd.)*
    built-in, *30-31*
        entertainment centers,
        148-149
        headboard, *22-23*
        shelves, *57, 59*
    for disabled persons, 79
    kitchen, *145*
Story-and-a-half houses, 98
    add-on options, 98, *99*
Streamlining, *32-33*
Stucco, 119, *120,* 120-121
Study, bedroom and, 22
Subcontractors, 140, 141
Subdivision of space, *22-23*
Sunspaces, *76-77*
Surface materials, exterior, 93,
    110-129
    masonry, *92,* 93, *118,* 119
        chart, *120,* 120-121
    roofing, 93, *126,* 127
        chart, *128,* 128-129
    siding. *See* Siding
Surface materials, interior
    floors, *154-155*
    walls and ceilings, *152-153*

T-Z

Table, drop-leaf, *28, 29*
Taxes, 136
Television rooms, *148-149*
Texture-111 (sand-spray)
    siding, 110, *112,* 112-113
Tile and slate, roofing,
    127, *128,* 128-129
Tile floors. *See* Floors: tile
Title I loans, FHA, 132, 133
Traffic patterns, 15
Two-story houses, 98
    add-on options, 98, *99*
Variances, gaining, 137
Veneers, masonry, *118,* 119
Vinyl siding, 10, *112,* 112-113
Walls
    freestanding, *22-23*
    insulating, *75*
    mirrors on, *19, 26-27, 37,*
    42-43
    porch conversions, 38
    removal, *42-43*
        in garage conversion,
        40-41
    surface materials
        interior, *152-153*

Walls *(contd.)*
    masonry, *92,* 93, *118,*
    119, *120,* 120-121
    See also Siding
Water in basement, solutions
    for, 37
Weight, visual, as space-
    stretching strategy, *18-19*
Wheelchair users, planning for,
    78-79
Windows
    additions, *82-83*
    arched, *48-49*
    bays, *60-61*
    with cathedral ceiling,
    52-53
    double-decker, *47*
    framing, *87*
    greenhouse style, for spa,
    146
    second-story, 102
    for unified effect, *50,*
    54-55
    wing extension, *56-57*
    in garage conversion, *40-41*
    Palladian, *12*
    skylights, *81, 97, 100-101,*
    142-143
    weatherproofing, *75*
Wing, house, extending, *56-57*
Wiring, 90, 141
Wood finishes, 122, *123*
    chart, *124,* 124-125
    for roofing, *126*
Wood flooring, 154-155, *155*
Wood shingles and shakes
    roofing, *126,* 127, *128,*
    128-129
    siding, 114, *116,* 116-117
Wood siding, natural, 114, *115*
    chart, *116,* 116-117
Wood wall/ceiling treatments,
    152-153
Working drawings, 72
Zones of house, 15
Zoning ordinances, 134
    variances, 137

Have BETTER HOMES AND
GARDENS® magazine
delivered to your door.
For information, write to:
MR. ROBERT AUSTIN
P.O. BOX 4536
DES MOINES, IA 50336